TAKING A CHANCE ON GOD

TAKING A CHANCE ON GOD

LIBERATING THEOLOGY
FOR GAYS, LESBIANS,
AND THEIR
LOVERS, FAMILIES,
AND FRIENDS

JOHN J. McNEILL

Beacon Press Boston

Beacon Press
25 Beacon Street
Boston, Massachusetts 02108

Beacon Press books
are published under the auspices of
the Unitarian Universalist Association of Congregations.

95 94 93 92 91 90 89   8 7 6 5 4 3 2

Text design by Hunter Graphics

Library of Congress Cataloging-in-Publication Data
McNeill, John J.
    Taking a chance on God : liberating theology for gays, lesbians, and
their lovers, families, and friends / John J. McNeill.
        p.
    Bibliography: p.
    ISBN 0-8070-7902-2   ISBN 0-8070-7903-3 (pbk.)
    1. Gays—religious life. 2. Homosexuality—religious aspects—
Christianity.   I. Title.
BV4596.G38M46   1988
208'.80664—dc 19   87-47875

I pray that
with God's merciful grace
this book may serve the spiritual good
of my lesbian sisters and gay brothers
and all who read it.

Contents

Contents

Preface

The question that has most often arisen concerning the relation of religion and sexuality is, What does our Christian faith (the Bible, tradition, current theological opinion) say about our human sexuality, its purposes, and how we ought to express it? There is a second question that is equally important, as James B. Nelson points out in his book *Between Two Gardens: Reflections on Sexuality and Religious Experience,*[1] namely, What does our experience as sexual human beings have to say about the way we do theology, read the Scriptures, interpret tradition, and attempt to live out the meaning of the Gospels?

There is a special need today for a *sexual theology,* as distinct from a theology about human sexuality. Our human sexuality has always played a vital role in our life of faith, but until now it has been hidden. Feminist theology has thrown a sharp light on the fact that most traditional theologies were based exclusively on a patriarchal view of reality.

Edmund Husserl, the father of phenomenology, observed that reality always speaks to us according to the question we pose to it. A person who is embodied as a female will thus ask radically different questions from those asked by someone embodied as a male. Consequently, the response each receives will also be radically different.

The premise of this book is that there are specific questions that lesbian women and gay men ask of reality that differ from heterosexual questions, and that there is thus a distinct contribution to be made to theology and spirituality from a gay perspective. This book, then, is an attempt to formulate that theology and spirituality from a gay perspective. I try to identify and discuss some of the principal realms of experience where lesbian and gay people, because of their sexual orientation, ask different questions, have different needs and, therefore, need to work out the special theological and spiritual implications that are rooted in the gay and lesbian experience.

Thomas E. Clarke, S.J., in his article "A New Way: Reflecting on Experience,"[2] writes of a new way of theologizing in the contemporary church, a way based primarily on "revelatory experience." Theology can no longer afford to be exclusively an a priori science that deduces conclusions from general principles; rather, it must take the form of an a posteriori science, drawing its conclusions from the empirical evidence present in people's lived experience. Clarke states that the agent and place of this new form of theological reflection are not the professional theologian in an academic setting but rather the members of the basic Christian community, in this case the lesbian and gay Christian community, who are trying to render an account to themselves and to others of their faith in order to inform their pastoral action. This process is described as "a common Christian reflection on revelatory experience (including especially the 'signs of the times') interpreted with the help of social analysis and on the basis of Scripture and tradition with a view to Christian action in the world."[3]

My intention in this book is to provide a spirituality based in the revelatory experience of lesbian and gay Christians, a spirituality designed to meet their special needs and inform their pastoral action in the world.

I also had in mind a more specific readership, one whose plight gives this book a special urgency: all my gay brothers who have AIDS or who are in danger of developing AIDS, as well as their lovers, families, and friends. These people have a desperate need to understand what they are going through in the context of a new spirituality that can allow them to relate their reality and experience as gay people and persons with AIDS to God's revelation of him/herself in Jesus.

This book took shape out of the thousands of hours I have spent as a psychotherapist sharing the pain and joy, struggles and triumphs of my lesbian and gay clients as they strove to put together their lives as both gay and Christian. The book grew further as I become aware of the basic patterns, both psychological and spiritual, that underlay my clients' struggles to win through to psychological health and spiritual maturity. It was also shaped by the scores of homilies, workshops, and retreats I have given for various gay groups, especially the retreats for lesbians and gays at Kirkridge Retreat Center in the Poconos.

This is a very personal book. Throughout I have drawn heavily on my own experience. I grew up as the youngest, gay son of a large Irish-American family in Buffalo, New York. My parents were hard-working people without much in the way of formal education. My mother had immigrated to this country from Ireland. Both my mother and father sincerely believed that the most precious treasure they had received from their parents, and which they in turn passed on to us, their children, was the gift of faith and hope.

My parents have been dead now for many years. My father was, and my mother would have been, proud of my call to priesthood and the religious life. Were they still alive, they might not have been able to comprehend the path I have followed, in obedience to what I believe is God's will, which led to my expulsion from the Society of Jesus and my loss of the legal right to exercise my priesthood. But I am confident that from their present perspective from within the kingdom of God, they can understand and agree with my desire to share the treasure of faith and hope they gave to me with my gay brothers and lesbian sisters.

I am also proud of my nearly forty years of membership in the Society of Jesus. I see the Jesuits as one of the greatest groups of men on earth, who are right now doing some of their most important work for human liberation, especially in Central and South America. Although I am legally separated from them, I shall always see myself as one with them in spirit.

My personal spirituality is based on the spiritual exercises of Saint Ignatius Loyola. Over the years I have worked in depth with many people of other Christian and non-Christian traditions. I have tried to uncover the pearl of spiritual insight that is universally applicable to the gay experience. The best way I know to arrive at these insights is to deepen my understanding and practice of my own tradition, and then share with others whatever I have found most valuable.

Ironically, the Vatican authorities can be thanked, at least in part, for helping to inspire this book. When they imprudently silenced me some twelve years ago on the issues of homosexuality and sexual ethics, and closed off my access to a teaching position at any Catholic school, they forced me to give up my career as a teacher and turn my attention to direct ministry to gay people and to the key spiritual issues that lesbians and gay men face.

Because my access to the classroom was cut off, I began a new career as a psychotherapist. My Jesuit superiors released me to do full-time ministry with gay people, and the Institutes of Religion and Health trained me as a therapist and enhanced my ability to perceive the linkage between issues of psychological growth and development, and spiritual growth and development.

Over the past twelve years I have been in a constant prayerful process of reflecting deeply on Scripture, in the hope that God would use me to bring a healing message, first of all to myself and then to my lesbian sisters and gay brothers. I have also been involved in reflecting deeply on psychodynamic processes and attempting to use my knowledge of those processes in order to bring about a healing of the psychic wounds of my gay clients.

Again, ironically, I have the Vatican authorities to thank for the opportunity to write and publish this book. When the Spirit led Vatican authorities recently to deny me the right to minister in any way to my gay sisters and brothers, they freed me from my ten-year silence by giving me an order that went beyond anything I could obey in good conscience. After over a year of prayer and consultation, I decided that my ultimate obedience was to God and for me to discontinue my ministry would have violated God's will for me.

This book, I hope, will contribute to the possibility of a new dimension of liberation theology. "The future of history," Gustavo Gutierrez writes, "belongs to the poor and the exploited. True liberation will be the work of the oppressed themselves; in them the Lord saves history. The spirituality of liberation will have as its basis the spirituality of the *anawim*."[4]

This book applies the three major themes of liberation theology—humanization; conscientization; and dialogue and community—to the gay and lesbian liberation movement. Humanization is the process whereby gay people develop a healthy self-identity and seek to be accepted and dealt with as subjects rather than objects. Conscientization is the process of becoming aware of the structures that oppress gay people. Dialogue and community represent the processes by which gay people develop their own social resources.

I hope this book will be given a careful and critical reading, not only by gays and lesbians, but also by all those interested in furthering the Gospel's objective of true human liberation. We gay people have a message of liberation not just for ourselves but for all humanity. The very process by which we free ourselves to accept our sexuality helps free everyone to accept their true selves.

I think it important to spell out the presuppositions of this book, especially its moral and theological presuppositions.[5] The present book rests on the theses proposed and defended in the book I published some twelve years ago, *The Church and the Homosexual*, recently republished in a revised and updated edition.[6] These theses have been denounced by some writers but have never seriously been challenged on a scholarly basis.

In *The Church and the Homosexual* I sought to refute three traditional stances taken by the Christian community regarding lesbian and gay relationships. I opposed, first of all, the view that God intends all human beings to be heterosexual, and that homosexuality therefore represents a deviation from God's divine plan—a deviation usually explained in terms of sin or, more recently, in terms of sickness. According to this view, those who find that they are lesbian or gay must change their orientation through prayer or counseling or, failing that, live totally celibate and sexually loveless lives. Sexual fulfillment thus becomes the exclusive right of heterosexuals. This is the position held in the Vatican letter "On the Pastoral Care of Homosexual Persons," issued in October 1986 to all the bishops of the world. This letter was deemed necessary to counter "deceitful propaganda" coming from gay Christian groups that were challenging the church's tradition and its interpretation of Scripture.

I suggested instead that God created human beings with a great variety of both gender identities and sexual-object choices. Consequently, the attempt to force humans into narrow heterosexist categories of "masculinity" or "femininity" can destroy the great richness and variety of God's creation.

In all cultures and in every period of history, a certain percentage of men and women develop as gays and lesbians. These individuals should be considered as part of God's creative plan.

Their sexual orientation has no necessary connection with sin, sickness, or failure; rather, it is a gift from God to be accepted and lived out with gratitude. God does not despise anything that God has created.

It should be stressed here, in opposition to certain current views, that human beings do not choose their sexual orientation; they discover it as something given. To pray for a change in one's sexual orientation is about as meaningful as to pray for a change in the color of one's eyes. Furthermore, there is no healthy way to reverse or change sexual orientation once it is established.

The claims of certain groups to be able to change homosexuals into heterosexuals has been shown to be spurious and frequently based in homophobia. The primary technique used to bring about this pseudo-change involves persuading gay people to internalize self-hatred, an approach that frequently causes great psychological harm and suffering. The Christian communities that resort to this kind of ministry usually do so to avoid any challenge to their traditional stance and to avoid any dialogue with self-accepting lesbians and gays and with professional psychotherapists. The real choice that faces lesbians and gays is not between heterosexuality and homosexuality, but between being able to form relationships and being cut off from any relational intimacy whatsoever.

Other churches have confined their official ministry to helping gay and lesbian people live out celibate lives. According to Christian tradition, celibacy is a special gift from God given to a certain few for the sake of God's kingdom. The occasional homosexual who receives this gift is indeed blessed. Roman Catholic clergy choose a celibate way of life voluntarily, but lay people who are homosexual are given no choice; they are told that they must be celibate their entire lives.

There is no reason to believe that God grants this gift to everyone who happens to be lesbian or gay. On the contrary, empirical studies have shown that the vast majority of gay people who have attempted to live a celibate life end up acting out their sexual needs in promiscuous and self-destructive ways. Every human being has a God-given right to sexual love and intimacy. Anyone who would deny that right to any individual must prove beyond all doubt the grounds for this denial. The only healthy and holy Christian response to a lesbian or gay orientation is to learn to accept it and live it out in a way that is consonant with Christian values.

The second thesis of *The Church and the Homosexual* was that homosexuals, rather than being a menace to the values of society and the family, as many have tended to assume, have, as a part of God's creative plan, special gifts and qualities and a very positive contribution to make to the development of society.[7] Indeed, if lesbians and gay men were to disappear, the further development of society toward greater humaneness would be seriously endangered. Consequently, I feel there is a special providence in the emergence of visible gay and lesbian communities within the Church at this point in history.

The third thesis of my earlier book was perhaps the most controversial. The church's traditional position has been that since every homosexual act is sinful and contrary to God's plan, the love that exists between gay and lesbian people is sinful and alienates the lovers from God. I argued that the love between two lesbians or gay men, assuming that it is a constructive human love, is *not* sinful, nor does it alienate the lovers from God's plan. On the contrary, it can be a holy love, mediating God's presence in the human community as effectively as heterosexual love.

I fully appreciate how controversial my arguments were, but I felt my position was supported by new evidence, coming from biblical studies and from various empirical studies in the human sciences, especially psychology and sociology, that completely undermined the traditional understanding of homosexuality as a chosen and changeable state. New insights into psychosexual development leave no doubt that one has no choice about sexual orientation and that the only healthy reaction to being lesbian or gay is to accept it. Above all else, there is the evidence that has come from the collective experience of lesbians and gays who, as committed Christians, are seeking to live their lives in conformity with Christian faith and values. All this evidence should give every Christian community serious reason to reconsider its understanding of homosexuality.

All the personal examples in this text are amalgrams of various clients, professional associates, and my own personal experiences. All situations have been disguised to ensure confidentiality.

I am very grateful to many people for making this book possible. First of all, I am grateful to all my gay and lesbian clients who did me the honor of trusting me enough to share their deepest joys and sorrows with me. I especially want to thank all those gay people with AIDS and those caring for persons with AIDS with whom I have worked for the past several years. If I have been able to share their many rich insights with the reader, it is only because they were willing to share their pain, fear, and sorrow, as well as their courage, joy, and hope in the face of adversity and death. A special word of gratitude goes to my training therapist, Arnold Rachman, for his skillful help.

I wish to acknowledge my indebtedness to all those who read the manuscript of this book and helped with its development, first of all Tom Fischer, who has done an extraordinary job of editing, and also Paul Hamilton, David Bailey, Norman Laurila, Margaret Kornfeld, Robert Svenson, Louis Swift, and Wilbert Sykes. I am also grateful to Robert Raines and Cynthia Hirni for the opportunity to develop many of these ideas at the Kirkridge Retreat Center. Finally, I want to thank my friend, Charles Chiarelli, whose daily support, encouragement, and assistance made the writing of this book possible.

Several weeks after the words "taking a chance on God" occurred to me as an appropriate title for this book, I suddenly realized where the phrase came from. Since the forties, I had always had an affection for a lovely ballad from the musical *Cabin in the Sky* entitled "Taking a Chance on Love." Scripture tells us that God is love, and whoever truly loves also knows God. I therefore believe that the statements "Taking a Chance on Love" and "Taking a Chance on God" are at some deep level identical, just as Jesus said that the commandment to love your neighbor is identical to the commandment to love God. So I looked up the lyrics of the song and found them surprisingly appropriate to the message of this book:

Taking a Chance on Love

I thought love's game was over,
lady luck had gone away.
I laid my cards on the table,
unable to play.
Then I heard good fortune say,
"They're dealing you a new hand today!"

Oh, here I go again,
I hear those trumpets blow again,
all aglow again,
taking a chance on love.

Here I slide again,
about to take that ride again,
starry-eyed again,
taking a chance on love.

I thought that cards were a frame-up
I never would try,
but now I'm taking the game up,
and the ace of hearts is high.

Things are mending now,
I see a rainbow blending now,
we'll have our happy ending now,
taking a chance on love.[8]

Part One

Growing Up in Our Faith: Spiritual Life and the Gay Experience

Introduction: Lesbians, Gays, and the Spiritual Life

Lesbians and gays have always been people of exceptional religious sensitivity. After many years of work as a psychoanalyst, Carl Jung made this observation concerning the spiritual life of his gay clients: "Often [gay people] are endowed with a wealth of religious feelings, which help [them] to bring the *ecclesia spiritualis* into reality, and a spiritual receptivity which makes them responsive to revelation."[1]

It is my experience as well, after working with hundreds of gay clients, that most lesbian and gay people are extraordinarily open to developing spiritual values. Mark Thompson's book *Gay Spirit: Myth and Meaning*[2] explores this spiritual aspect of the gay and lesbian community. Very often the spiritual leadership of the human community as a whole comes from its lesbian and gay members. Yet this very openness leaves gay people particularly vulnerable to the pathological aspects of religion.

In part 1, I shall discuss the mature and immature forms that faith can take in gay spiritual life. Next, I examine the phenomenon of gay atheism and the frequently healthy spiritual role that gay atheism can play. Finally, I focus on one of the main challenges faced by most of my lesbian and gay clients who are trying to develop a spiritual life, namely, the importance of discerning the difference between pathological and healthy systems of belief. Continuing to hold on to a pathological belief system that has been deeply embedded in the unconscious results in feelings of fear, guilt, and shame, and in many cases has been both the primary source of resistance to psychological healing and the principal obstacle to spiritual maturity.

1

Developing a Mature Faith Life

God's gift was not a spirit of timidity, but the Spirit of power and love and self-control.

2 Timothy 1:7

The painful experience of being an exile takes myriad forms for a gay or lesbian person. One that I experienced myself was being a gay soldier and veteran. Lesbians and gay men who loved and served their country courageously in the armed forces have suffered a special injustice because they faced the awful threat of being court-martialed and dishonorably discharged if their sexual orientation ever became known, in spite of their loyal and courageous service.

Recently, an incident occurred that reminded me once again of the pain of our exiled state. A few years ago a local court refused gay veterans permission to march under their banner in a veterans' parade. That decision was later reversed by a higher court, but the first time gay veterans marched a fanatic attacked their banner with a knife.

Shortly after my ordination in 1960, I had the opportunity to journey back to the battlefields in Europe where my infantry division, the 87th, went into combat in the fall of 1944. I looked up all the names of my former friends and comrades who had fallen in battle and offered mass in their memory.

When I preached to a group of gay veterans twenty-five years later on Veterans' Day, 1985, I wore my wartime decorations in the pulpit: the Combat Infantryman Badge, the Purple Heart, and the Good Conduct Badge. I normally object to symbols of patriotism in the sanctuary, because I believe strongly that when we stand before God, we must stand in solidarity with all humanity, as Jesus did. We should not try to approach God when we stand exclusively with only some portion of humanity: our own family, race, ethnic group, or countrymen. I decided to wear those medals as a protest against injustice.

I enlisted in the army during the Second World War when I was seventeen years old. I served in combat with the 87th Infantry division in the Third Army under General George Patton of "our blood, his guts" fame, whose body now lies at rest at the head of a graveyard full of dead soldiers in a military cemetery in Luxembourg. I went overseas as a private and served as a foot soldier carrying a bandalier of mortar shells on my back into the combat zone in Alsace-Lorraine. On December 2, 1944, my company was one of the first to penetrate the German border. Shortly thereafter we were surrounded by tiger tanks and all the soldiers in my platoon were either killed or captured.

I will never forget the terror I experienced when I realized that a tank had us pinned down in a German foxhole we had taken earlier, so that we could not return fire. At that moment a German soldier was making the classic infantry maneuver of crawling up to within throwing range to toss a rolling-pin-style hand grenade into our foxhole. We stood up, our hands high in the air. Sure enough, a German soldier, grenade in hand, stood up about twenty feet away and ordered us down the hill. We were *Kriegsgefangenen,* prisoners of war.

Even now, some forty-three years later, I can see myself, a frightened eighteen-year-old, being led down a dirt road with a rifle at my back. At a crossroads we came upon a wayside shrine, a cross with the body of Christ on it. In the broken German I had learned as a freshman at Canisius College in Buffalo, I asked the guard for permission to say a prayer. I remember kneeling and making what I thought would be my last Act of Contrition, since I was convinced that I was going to be shot. In the meantime, the guard leaned on his rifle and smoked one of my cigarettes.

Well, obviously I was not shot; I was led away to a central collection point for prisoners. There followed six months of terror, starvation, and beatings, but, thanks be to God, I survived and I'm still here. I remember my prayer then was, "Lord, I am too young to die; let me live to do your work." That prayer was certainly heard.

One of the issues we who survived have to deal with is survivor's guilt. Why were we chosen to live while so many others died? There is an impenetrable mystery in that question. I emerged from prison camp with a new understanding of my faith, and after about two years of hospitalization and medication I regained my health in both mind and body and finally, in 1948, I entered the novitiate of the Society of Jesus in order to do God's work on earth, "Ad Majorem Dei Gloriam," to the greater glory of God. Every moment from that day to this was borrowed time, which I believe was given to me because there was a task that God wanted me to achieve in this life.

That young man who knelt and prayed at the wayside cross obviously had received the gift of faith, the most precious inheritance his parents passed on to him. The apostle Paul, speaking of our faith, tells us: "God's gift was not a spirit of timidity, but the Spirit of power and love and self-control" (2 Tm. 1:7).

But my faith still had a long journey ahead, with many trials to undergo and many idols to be smashed. It is important for us to be aware that our religious faith needs to grow up and mature, just as we grow up and mature in all other aspects of our lives. This is a process that continues until we die. There are aspects of our faith that are healthy and favorable to growth; there are other aspects that are neurotic and destructive. We are all called on to be aware of the state of our faith, to strengthen what is healthy in it and to diminish what is sick and neurotic.

For example, there was a time when I confused the voice of God with my own sadistic superego. I allowed my spiritual life to be permeated by neurotic guilt. My spirit became a spirit of cowardice, not a spirit of power and love. It took me a long time to dispel that guilt, and the process is still going on. Only gradually did I come to realize the meaning of Saint Iranaeus's famous statement, *Gloria Dei, homo vivens*—the glory of God is humans fully alive. I thought God's glory was to be found only in suffering and not in moments of pleasure or joy.

It is also possible to confuse faith with a need for security. One example of this is the immature belief that one can only discover the will of God in the pronouncements of external authorities. It can be very tempting to submit blindly to the voice of authority and then, like some latter-day Eichmann, disclaim any responsibility for the consequences of our obedience. But if we do so we fail to see that God can speak to us directly through our own experience. There may be times when, in order to accomplish what God wants, we may have to oppose authority and take full responsibility for the consequences of our choices and actions.

The most serious distortion of faith of which I have been guilty is the belief that I somehow had to *earn* God's grace and love through what I accomplished. At such times I failed to see that it is not necessary to earn God's love, that in the end, like life itself, all is a gift. God gives his/her gifts freely, and the only meaningful response is gratitude.

What was it that I needed in order to arrive at a healthy and mature faith? It was a healing of my vision of God. Let me speak of my own spiritual journey within the gay spiritual community, and especially as a member of Dignity, over the past fifteen years.

I grew up in a homophobic neighborhood in Buffalo, New York. Because I was aware of my sexual feelings, I was tormented by the fear that, at the very heart of my being, there was a fatal flaw that rendered me defective and unlovable. I thought that I could be accepted by my family and Church only if I could hide, deny, and repress the specific form that my ability to love and sexual feelings had taken. With the full support of a homophobic Church, I transferred my fear of rejection to God, and in so doing built up a false image of God. I became a masochistic worshiper of the God created by my own superego.

At the same time I unconsciously built up a rage against that God, a rage against the injustice of being rejected for something over which I had no choice. But fear of God led me to suppress that rage. I remember reciting the Act of Contrition after confession: "O my God, I am heartily sorry for having offended thee, because I dread the loss of heaven and the pains of hell. . . ." I could identify with the fear contained in those words. The words went on, but my feelings did not: "but most of all because I have offended thee, my God, who art all good and deserving of all my love." Love and rage could not coexist in my heart.

I began to act out that rage in self-destructive ways. Out of a sense of fear, I tried to sacrifice my deepest reality, my ability to feel and to love, in order to be acceptable to that God. Like the pagans of old who out of fear would cast their firstborn into the fire before the statue of Baal, I too thought I had to sacrifice a vital part of myself in order to be acceptable to God. I was truly blind to God's reality, and worshiped an idol of my own making.

I remember well an incident that occurred right after my ordination to the priesthood. I had looked forward for many long years to that event. We Jesuits have a tendency to regard ordination as a reward for a well-spent life. The day after my ordination at Fordham University by Cardinal Spellman, the re-alization hit me that I was obliged under pain of mortal sin to recite the Holy Office, at that time still in Latin, several times a day—an obligation that seemed to me extremely burdensome to carry out. I immediately went into a deep depression. Here was another daily occasion to commit more mortal sins!

Returning to Woodstock Seminary from my first mass in Buffalo, I met a priest friend on the train. He told me the latest joke making the rounds of clerical circles in Washington. It was about three priests who ended up in hell. The first priest, Peter, said to the second priest, Joe, "Joe, why are you here?" Joe answered, "I got what I deserved. I ran off with the parish money, lived riotously in Miami, and I was killed in a car crash without repenting or making restitution." He asked Peter in turn, "Why are you here?" Peter answered, "Well, I got what I deserved. I kept a mistress in an apartment behind the parish house and I died in bed with her, unrepentant." Then they both turned to the third priest, Pat, and said, "Pat! Why are you here? You were the ideal priest. You had that poor parish in the inner city. You worked day and night with the poor in the soup kitchen. We thought you were a saint." Pat answered, "Well, I got what I deserved. The last night of my life I was very tired after eighteen hours of work with the poor; so I skipped the final hour of the office and died in my sleep. So here I am!"

As soon as I heard that joke, God gave me the grace to realize that reading the Holy Office was the wrong kind of worship for me. I decided to take a chance on God. I put my breviary aside and have not read it as an obligation since. This has not had the slightest effect on my delight in the Holy Office when I am on retreat or when I join the monks at Mount Saviour Monastery in singing God's praise. That experience helped me to grasp a primary principle of healthy, mature spiritual life: resist and refuse to perform any religious observance that is based exclusively on fear of God!

Today we gay people have a desperate need for a healthy and adult faith; a faith built directly on our own experience; a faith that can lead us to reach out in love to each other, rather than selfishly seek our own security; a faith strong enough to overcome all fears, especially fear of death.

The threat of AIDS can cause us to fall back into immature, neurotic faith. Neurotic faith is based in fear and a spirit of cowardice. In the chapters that follow I will attempt to spell out many of the forms that neurotic faith can take and what we must do to live out our lives as gay people with a healthy commitment to life and to each other.

The supreme gift of God is love. To experience genuine human love, to be part of a community of love is to experience the presence of God. However, love is paradoxical. It is absolutely necessary for a happy, fulfilled human life. And it is absolutely impossible by human means alone. That is why John could write, "Anyone who fails to love can never have known God, because God is love" (1 Jn. 4:8).

Love is always a miracle; always God's gift of self; always an experience of the divine. In the community of love to which we belong, we daily experience the presence of God. This is an experience we freely receive, and one that we can, if we wish, out of gratitude freely give to others in return.

I would like to end this reflection on the mature life of faith with the eyewitness account of a gay priest who was beaten to death in a German concentration camp during World War II because he refused to stop praying or to express contempt for himself. The story is recounted by Heinz Heger in his book *The Men with the Pink Triangle,* in which he recalls what took place in the special concentration camp for gay men in Sachsenhausen (Sachsenhausen was a "level 3" camp where prisoners were deliberately worked to death):

Toward the end of February, 1940, a priest arrived in our block, a man some 60 years of age, tall and with distinguished features. We later discovered that he came from Sudetenland, from an aristocratic German family. He found the torment of the arrival procedure especially trying, particularly the long wait naked and barefoot outside the block. When his tonsure was discovered after the shower, the SS corporal in charge took up a razor and said: "I'll go to work on this one's head myself, and extend his tonsure a bit." And he shaved the priest's head with the razor, taking little trouble to avoid cutting the scalp. Quite the contrary.

The priest returned to the day-room of our block with his head cut open and blood streaming down. His face was ashen and his eyes stared uncomprehendingly into the distance. He sat down on a bench, folded his hands in his lap and said softly, more to himself than to anyone else: "And yet man is good, he is a creature of God!"

I was sitting beside him, and said softly but firmly: "Not all men; there are also beasts in human form, whom the devil must have made."

The priest paid no attention to my words, he just prayed silently, merely moving his lips. I was deeply moved, even though I was by then already numbed by all the suffering I had so often seen, and indeed experienced myself. But I had always had a great respect for priests, so that his silent prayer, this mute appeal to God, whom he called on for help and strength in his bodily pain and mental torment, went straight to my heart.

Our block Capo, however, a repulsive and brutal "green," must have reported the priest's praying to the SS, for our block sergeant suddenly burst into the day-room accompanied by a second NCO, seizing the terrified priest from the bench and punching and insulting him. The priest bore the beating and abuse without complaint, and just stared at the two SS men with wide, astonished eyes. This must simply have made them angrier, for they now took one of the benches and tied the priest to it.

They started to beat him indiscriminately with their sticks, on his stomach, his belly and his sexual organs. They seemed to get more and more ecstatic, and gloated: "We'll drive the praying out of you! You bum-fucker! bum-fucker!"

The priest collapsed into unconsciousness, was shaken awake and then fell unconscious again.

Finally the two SS sadists ceased their blows and left the day-room, though not without scornfully calling back to the man they had now quite destroyed: "OK, you randy old rat-bag, you can piss with your arse-hole in future."

The priest just rattled and groaned. We released him and laid him on his bed. He tried to raise his hand in thanks, but he hadn't the strength, and his voice gave out when he tried to say "thank you." He just lay without stirring, his eyes open, each movement contorting his face with pain.

I felt I was witnessing the crucifixion of Christ in modern guise. Instead of Roman soldiers, Hitler's SS thugs, and a bench instead of a cross. The torment of the Saviour, however, was scarcely greater than that inflicted on one of his representatives nineteen hundred years later here in Sachsenhausen.

The next morning, when we marched to the parade-ground, we had almost to carry the priest, who seemed about to collapse again from pain and weakness. When our block senior reported to the SS block sergeant, the latter came over to the priest and shouted: "Can't you stand up, you arse-hole," adding: "You filthy queer, you filthy swine, say what you are!" The priest was supposed to repeat the insults, but no sound came from the lips of the broken man. The SS man angrily fell on him and was about to start beating him once again.

Suddenly the unimaginable happened, something that is still inexplicable to me and that I could only see as a miracle, the finger of God.

From the overcast sky, a sudden ray of sunshine that illuminated the priest's battered face.

Out of the thousands of assembled prisoners, only him, and at the very moment when he was going to be beaten again. There was a remarkable silence, and all present stared fixedly at the sky, astonished by what had happened. The SS sergeant himself looked up at the clouds in wonder for a few seconds, then let his hand raised for a beating, sink slowly to his side, and walked wordlessly away to take up his position at the end of our ranks.

The priest bowed his head and murmured with a dying voice: "Thank you Lord . . . I know that my time has come . . ."

He was still with us for the evening parade. But we no longer needed to carry him, we laid him down at the end of the line with the other dead of the day, so that our numbers should be complete for the roll-call—no matter whether living or dead.[1]

We gays and lesbians have a model and a patron in this anonymous priest who was martyred because he dared to be both gay and a man of prayer.

Almighty God, help us, your lesbian daughters and gay sons, to grow and mature in our faith. Free us from the spirit of fear and cowardice. Grant that all the suffering and pain experienced in the past by those who were persecuted because they were gay or lesbian will not have been in vain, but will help win for us and for all our people in the future the grace of true liberation. Fill our hearts with a deep awareness of your love for us so that we may be free to love one another in a spirit of gratitude. Amen.

2

The Challenge of Gay Atheism

The people that lived in darkness has seen a great light; on those who dwell in the land and shadow of death a light has dawned.

Matthew 4:16

The editor of a major gay publication recently wrote that he saw religion as the enemy of humanity. He expressed astonishment that gay people still go to church, and felt that their loyalty to their church represented either incredible courage or incredible stupidity. The same paper ran an article entitled "A Gay Atheist League Says Good-bye to God: Gay Atheists Come Out." In that article, a former member of Dignity who is one of the founders of the league says of Dignity: "I never got anything out of it. I thought Dignity would never change the Church. . . ." What I would like to deal with here is the question, What should our response as gay believers be to this challenge?

As we recall the revelation of God's love for all humanity as manifest in Jesus, let us reflect for a moment on all our atheist brothers and sisters. It is important, first of all, to make a distinction between those who have left the human church (frequently for good reasons) but have retained their faith in God, and those who have utterly given up their faith in God.

I am acutely aware of the pain and despair that lie behind so many lesbian and gay defections from religious belief. I am aware of many hundreds of gay people who have impoverished their lives, depriving themselves of their religious inheritance and cutting off the light of God's love, because of their anger at the humanly fallible church. When many of my clients began therapy, they felt trapped by an unresolvable dilemma: to believe in God necessarily seemed to involve hating their own gayness, and accepting their gayness seemed to involve rejecting their faith in God. One of the most important breakthroughs they made in therapy was the realization that God is not identical with any particular church.

We must all mature in our faith to the point where we can separate our faith in God from the human and fallible church. We must develop our personal life of prayer so that we have our own direct and immediate contact with God. We can no longer allow our faith and belief to depend exclusively on the mediation of the church, with the result that if we become disillusioned with and scandalized by the human church, we are tempted to give up all belief. We must take a chance on God, keeping in mind that God, too, may well be scandalized by the church. After all, during his lifetime Jesus was in serious conflict with his church and its authorities.

What can we who continue in our faith learn from our atheist friends? When we encounter a nonbeliever, our prime duty is to scrutinize ourselves. We must ask ourselves as Christians to what extent God is a living, vital reality for us. As the late Gabriel Marcel, the French Catholic philosopher, put it: "The believer must see him- or herself as someone responsible in a certain measure for the unbelief of the other. . . . Were God to manifest himself through us as a light shining through a transparent covering, then He would impose himself on our interlocutor."

This is the challenge that our atheist brothers and sisters pose to those of us who are lesbian and gay believers: we must become a community of love. We must ask God to empower us to manifest God's love to our atheist brothers and sisters. The pagans were struck by the intensity of unselfish love present in the early Christian communities. And because of the attractiveness of that love, they wanted to join and take part. We must let the light of God's love shine through us, so that our atheist colleagues may have the chance to experience through us, not only the fact that God exists, but that God truly loves them as gay and lesbian persons.

There is another lesson that we can learn from our gay atheist colleagues. As Pope Paul VI put it in an Easter address to all the atheists of the world:

> Perhaps many in your midst have ideas about religion that are inaccurate and inadmissible. Perhaps for them faith is taken to be exactly what it is not: an offense to reason, an obstacle to progress, a humiliation for humans, a sadness for life. Perhaps some of them are more apt to welcome the burst of light. For, unless they are asleep in laziness and ignorance, the darkness of atheism dilates the pupils of their eyes in a painful effort to decipher obscurely the meaning and the why of life and destiny.

We who believe must ask ourselves to what extent we have presented our faith as an offense to human reason, an obstacle to progress, a humiliation for humans, and a sadness for life. Insofar as we are still worshiping the god of fear created by our superegos, our atheist friends are right to keep their distance. My experience is that most atheists are involved in an unconscious effort to purify the concept of God and destroy idols. If they could clarify on a conscious level the nature of the God they refuse to believe in, I believe that most of us would agree with them in refusing that god our belief and worship. We must listen to our atheist critics. They are very quick to pick up the neurotic and immature aspects of our faith.

I believe there is a necessary atheistic stage in the psychic development of lesbians and gays. This is comparable to the stage in theological thinking known as the *via negativa*, the "negative path." For most of my clients the idea of God became so identified with homophobic self-hatred that the only way they could deal with God was to take a vacation from religion while they dealt with the processes of coming out and accepting themselves. Only after they had a secure, positive self-image were they able to make a critical return to the question of religious belief.

Frequently we use our religion as a security blanket, as insurance against an uncertain future, rather than as a challenge to grow and realize all our creative potential. Frequently we remain children, passive and irresponsible, looking to see what we can get out of religion rather than offering what we can give. We sometimes use our religion to get God *out* of our lives rather than to put God *into* our lives.

We lesbian and gay believers must ask for the grace to be intensely aware that in all human encounters God is present. We must keep in mind Mary's *fiat:* Let what you have said be done to me. It lies in our power to put God into our lives or to deny God's presence. God will be in our lives insofar as we are ready to live lives of unselfish love as a response of gratitude for the love God has shown us in Jesus.

May the awareness and the experience of God's love for you as lesbian women and gay men fill you with joy and transform you into apostles of love. Amen.

3

Pathological Religion
and Healthy Religion

I am Yahweh your God who brought you out of . . . the house of slavery.
You shall have no gods except me.

Exodus 20:1–3

Gay and lesbian people have a special need to be able to discern the difference between pathological and healthy religious belief systems, since they are easily victimized by pathological religion.[1] When pathological belief systems and feelings become rooted deep in the unconscious of gay people, the result can be resistance to healthy self-acceptance.

Like everything else relating to human beings, systems of religious belief reflect our psychological health or its lack. One of the best studies of the differences in religious belief between healthy families and families with serious psychological illness is W. Robert Beavers's *Psychotherapy and Growth: A Family Systems Perspective*.[2] This book, based on a long-term empirical study, divided the families into three groups: severely dysfunctional, mid-range, and optimal. The distinctions were based on the degree of mental illness present in the family and on its level of functioning. For example, families were labeled severely dysfunctional if one or more members were frequently hospitalized for mental breakdowns. Optimal families, on the other hand, were those in which there was no trace of mental illness.

One of the many variables Beavers dealt with in evaluating families was the role of "transcendent values," which normally took the form of traditional religious belief. Underlying these values was the ability of family members to adapt to the inevitable losses that result from growth, development, aging, and death.

Healthy families must be able to self-destruct. Children grow up, leave home, and become self-sufficient adults. Parents grow old, experience physical decline, become ill, and die. A great deal of family pathology has to do with the denial of these realities. The inability of parents to let go of their children or children's inability to let go of their parents is usually related to a refusal to accept our own mortality. Both are a form of denial of death.

Every culture must provide a set of "mythic" truths, a belief system, that touches every member of society, drawing them together into a whole by giving them a group identity and providing some form of trusting relationship between the individual and a benign universe. A healthy system of transcendent values allows family members to center themselves in the universe and define their activities as meaningful without depending on unchanging family relationships. Most frequently, families achieve this kind of centering through conventional religion. But often the belief system reflects the needs and convictions of the individual and incorporates various humanitarian goals along with transcendent values. In any case, some form of value system that transcends the security of the family itself is absolutely necessary in order to achieve psychic health.

According to Beavers, the most significant lesson that emerged from his study is that within optimal families the ability to accept loss is associated with a system of transcendent values that provides hope, trust, and meaning when human helplessness threatens to become overwhelming. As Robert Browning put it, there is only one serious question in life: Can we love on condition that the one we love must die? We are all painfully aware of the relationship between intimacy and our consciousness of human finitude and death.

The primary issue concerning religious belief systems, from a therapeutic viewpoint, is not whether they are "true" or "false," but whether they provide a support system that allows healthy development in the individual and in the family; or do the belief systems themselves operate in such a way that they are a source of pathology?

A traditional religious belief is that "grace builds on nature," in other words, religious life depends on a good foundation in human health. Therefore, we can legitimately evaluate the validity of a religious belief system by its psychological consequences. Good theology will result in good psychology, and vice versa. Accordingly, bad theology will have negative psychological consequences. This is nothing more than an application of the biblical norm: "You will be able to tell them by their fruits" (Mt. 7:16). If, as Saint Irenaeus proclaimed, the glory of God is humans fully alive, then clearly a belief system that results in the destruction of human health cannot serve the glory of God.

The empirical evidence provided by family studies also gives us a way to evaluate religious belief systems. For example, if a religious belief system acknowledges and offers support for both individual choice and for human limits and vulnerability, then it is compatible with the rule system of an optimal family. On the other hand, belief systems that discourage individual choice and decision making; that impose rules and beliefs authoritatively; that leave no room for personal discovery; that encourage obedience through fear of punishment or rejection; that encourage a hopeless quest for perfection, especially by demanding a total repression of all sexuality or feelings of anger; and, finally, that discourage the validation of ego-skills through a false understanding of humility—these systems predominate in severely dysfunctional families and indicate that there is something basically wrong with the way that belief system operates.

Part of the therapeutic process for lesbians and gays who come from a religious background should be to bring into full awareness all hidden belief systems with their accompanying feelings of shame and low self-esteem, so that they can be challenged by the healthy religious values of the conscious ego.

The distinction between pathological and healthy religion cuts across all denominational boundaries. Any given denomination or sect can elicit pathological or healthy responses from its members. The influence of parents is also crucial. There is a direct connection between the kind of parenting a person had and the degree to which that individual's religious beliefs are healthy or pathological. Those who have had good, loving parents will be open to a liberating message of love from their religion. Loving parents can "defang the poison of religion," and allow children to receive only its benefits. In contrast, children of unloving parents will tend to create for themselves an unloving God whom they obey out of fear.

Pathological religion has much in common with the severely dysfunctional family. It relies on fear of punishment to obtain obedience; it uses guilt as a subtle lever for manipulation and control. It fears freedom and cultivates blind, unquestioning obedience. Even normal doubts are punished and repressed because they are seen as threatening. Pathological religion and families always define themselves in terms of what they are against, and are unclear about what they are for. They both see enemies on every side: the media, humanists, communists, intellectuals, feminists, gays, do-gooders, etc.

As an illustration of a pathological interpretation of religious faith, consider this advertisement, sponsored by the Knights of Columbus Religious Information Bureau. The advertisement appeared originally on October 24, 1965, in the *New York Herald Tribune* (this date was just before the opening of the Second Vatican Council):

What Faith Does for the Catholic Man!

He sees in his religion, first of all, a means to the salvation of his immortal soul.

But it also has a more immediate and urgent purpose— to teach him *how to live!*

The Catholic man doesn't have to invent his own theory as to the nature of God. He doesn't have to set up his own code of ethics for his relations with other men. He doesn't have to formulate personal standards of moral and social behavior . . . or make his own distinctions between right and wrong, good and bad.

All these problems are resolved for him by his belief in God's revealed truth . . . by the clear instructions found in the gospel of Jesus Christ . . . by his acceptance of the Sacraments dispensed through the Church for the nourishment of his soul. . . .

I find this understanding of the Catholic faith definitely pathological. Leaving aside the ad's failure to mention the Christian message of Resurrection and the implicit sexism of its exclusive appeal to men, the Catholic faith is identified here with total immaturity, passivity, blind faith, and obedience. We are urged not to think or reflect or use any of our God-given skills, but to accept, blindly and without question, directives from above. The Christian depicted here is one who sees his or her only duty as giving blind obedience and who does not accept responsibility for the consequences of his or her actions.

Fortunately, the distortions of faith in this advertisement were corrected in many of the documents of Vatican II. For example, in the document "The Church in the Modern World," lay people are urged to accept their responsibility to apply Christian principles in the areas of their expertise. They are told not to look for or expect definitive directives from the church or the priesthood, since that is not their task. Rather, every individual has the inalienable duty in conscience to search out how Christian values apply in his or her life.

Recent pronouncements from Rome and the local hierarchy seem to indicate a desire to set the church back and return to a totally authoritarian religion, one that denies lay people, and even professional theologians, any right to judge how religious principles can be applied to the complex problems of modern life.

This kind of religious belief seems to reflect the pathological mind set and insecurity of the severely dysfunctional family, and suggests that the present state of the church hierarchy, especially in Rome, is plagued by a pathological insecurity concerning their power and authority and the very existence of the Roman bureaucracy. Consequently, they are trying to impose an authoritarian rule on the whole church, a rule that is inimical to the psychic health and growth of the faithful. Let us all pray to God to send the Holy Spirit, so palpably present at the Second Vatican Council, once again to heal the fears and insecurity of our church leaders and free them again to risk growth and change.

A much-cited text in the New Testament has frequently been misinterpreted in a pernicious way. In Matthew 5:48, Jesus is reported as saying: "You must therefore be perfect just as your heavenly Father is perfect." The passage is sometimes interpreted as demanding a kind of moral perfection that is impossible for humans to achieve. Gays and lesbians are particularly susceptible to being caught up in the pursuit of an unobtainable perfection as a way of compensating for their difference. But the Greek word used in the original text, *teleios,* does not imply moral perfection. The term, as used by Aristotle and other Greek philosophers, derives from biology and describes an organism that has come to its full potential; for example, an oak tree that has reached maturity is the *teleios* of an acorn. What we are being told then, is that we must become what God intended us to be. We must become self-realized, as God is. Paul uses the same word when he exhorts us to come to the same fullness of mature humanity which was to be found in Jesus. The healthy implication of this text for gay people is that God wants them to become precisely what they are: healthy, mature lesbian women and gay men.

We lesbian and gay believers have the right and the duty to carefully scrutinize all religious belief systems and distinguish between those belief systems that support our need to achieve healthy self-acceptance and those that are destructive of our psychic health and maturity.

Almighty God, send your Spirit of love to help us lesbians and gays discern what is healthy and what destructive in our personal belief system. Help us to courageously confront our church whenever we find it acting in a way harmful to our well-being and psychic health. Amen.

4

Spiritual Maturity: A Challenge for Lesbian and Gay Christians

This is what Yahweh asks of you: only this, to act justly, to love tenderly and to walk humbly with your God.

Micah 6:8

A primary task of gay religious groups as they seek to foster the spiritual growth of their members is to teach us how to become self-centered in a healthy way, so that we are able to take responsibility before God and our fellow humans for our own choices and our own lives. We must learn that we cannot live our lives simply to meet the expectations of others, whether those others are parents or church officials.

As lesbian women and gay men, we must prayerfully undertake a personal reevaluation of what we have inherited, because much of what has come down to us from the church has been contaminated by the evil of homophobia. We must ask ourselves which of the church's values we continue to want, respect, and love; in other words, which values are compatible with who we are and are not destructive of our dignity as persons. As I mentioned earlier, whatever is psychologically destructive must be bad theology. Thus our identification of the destructive elements will be a service to the church, helping it to separate purely human traditions from the authentic word of God.

The self-centering and maturing process has a basis in God's revelation in Scripture. Pentecost, the coming of the Holy Spirit, was the last in a series of epiphanies or revelations of God that had been going on for millennia. When the followers of Moses began to worship God in the image of a golden calf—a worship that necessarily involved a dehumanization and depersonalization of the self, and a regression back into the subhuman, God revealed him/herself as a person. The central message of that revelation was that God is a person and that we give God true worship primarily through the development of our specifically human capacities for work, joy, play, and love.

The progressive revelation of God's self as Father, Son, and Holy Spirit represents a progressive identification with and interiorization of the divine presence in our lives. In the first stage, God appears as a parent figure, one who establishes laws and demands obedience, and yet a parent who is also faithful, compassionate, and forgiving. In the second stage of this self-revelation, God becomes present to us as a fellow human being in the figure of Jesus, our brother and fellow human. At this stage God is still outside us, but is more accessible to us in the human form of Jesus. In the last stage God appears as the Holy Spirit of love who now dwells within us. As the prophet Jeremiah stated, the old covenant with God was based on the law and the external authority of God: "I had to show them who was master" (Jr. 31:32). However, the new covenant is essentially different. In the new covenant, Jeremiah predicts, God will write the law deep within us, on our hearts. As a result every human being, from the least to the greatest, will be able to find the will of God within him- or herself and his or her experience:

This is the covenant I will make with the House of Israel when those days arrive—it is Yahweh who speaks. Deep within them I will plant my Law, writing it on their hearts. Then I will be their God and they shall be my people. There will be no further need for neighbor to try to teach neighbor, or brother to say to brother, "Learn to know Yahweh!" No, they will all know me, the least no less than the greatest—it is Yahweh who speaks—since I will forgive their iniquity and never call their sin to mind. (Jr. 31:33–34)

At one point in his discourse at the Last Supper, Jesus said to his disciples: "It is for your own good that I am going, because unless I go, the Advocate will not come to you." (Jn. 16:7). Why did Jesus have to disappear from our midst in order that the Spirit of the new covenant could become present? As long as Jesus remained present among the apostles, they had their center of authority and guide outside themselves. They were trying to meet the expectations of someone else. As long as they remained under the personal authority of Jesus, they were still children. They had not yet become fully creative and responsible adults.

With the death and resurrection of Jesus and the coming of the Holy Spirit, however, the apostles received a challenge as well as an opportunity to mature. They had to give up the security and the comfort of a provident leader. From that time on, they had to find the will of God within themselves. It was only after the coming of the Spirit that the apostles found the courage to leave the security of the upper room and go forth into the world as creative and responsible agents of the Spirit. My prayer and hope is that the lesbian and gay religious community will receive the grace from the Holy Spirit to be able to leave its closet and go forth courageously to encounter the church and the world with absolute confidence in its mission.

In some sense, each of us has to recapitulate the maturing process that the apostles went through. As children, we necessarily tend to understand God primarily in the image of a parental figure. As young men and women we can relate to Jesus as our brother and model. However, as adults, we begin to relate to God primarily through the indwelling Spirit of love.

There is a tendency in our spiritual lives, however, to remain immature, to always want to be children—passive, obedient, or rebellious, but in any case irresponsible. Although we may occasionally allow ourselves a healthy regression into childhood, it is the destiny of every child to grow up. We must leave the family into which we were born, leave father and mother, and form our own community.

So too in our spiritual lives we should all pass from a passive, irresponsible role to an active and creative role in our spiritual community. The gay and lesbian Christian community has a special need for mature, self-motivated, autonomous leaders: leaders who are capable of discernment, who can be creatively angry, who are capable of relating to the church as critical lovers and loving critics.

The gay and lesbian Christian community represents an attempt to build a spiritual community of love: first of all self-love, then love for our lesbian sisters and gay brothers, and finally love for the church and a desire to free it from its sexist, heterosexist enslavement. But all true love is a special grace, a gift from God. Consequently, to do the work that the gay religious movement proposes to do, there is an absolute need for spiritual strength, for God's help.

I do not believe it is an accident that the gay and lesbian religious community came into existence in the same decade in which there was an extraordinary outpouring of the gifts of the Holy Spirit. We need to be a charismatic community of prayer. We need the confirmation of hearing God speak to us directly. We who are lesbian or gay have a special need for the gifts of the Spirit. We need a direct experience of God's love in order to receive the Spirit of reconciliation at the deepest levels of our being, in order to be able to accept and love ourselves, to accept and love each other, to believe and accept God's love for and acceptance of us at the very moment others in the church condemn us in God's name.

Above all we need a spirit of prayer. We must think, live, work, and play in the presence of God. We must lead all our thoughts out of their fearful isolation into a fearless conversation with God. Understandably, there is a deep resistance to making ourselves so vulnerable, so naked, so totally unprotected. We want to love God; we also want to keep a little corner of our inner life for ourselves alone, so we can hide in the closet. The same fears that frequently keep us from being intimate with each other keep us from being intimate with God. My hope is that we will receive the grace to be able to break down some of the barriers that prevent us from being open to God and, as a result, prevent us from being open to ourselves, each other, and the world.

Listen to the promise God made through the prophet Isaiah to those who work for the liberation of the oppressed:

Is not this the sort of fast that pleases me
—it is the Lord Yahweh who speaks—
to break unjust fetters
and undo the thongs of the yoke,

to let the oppressed go free
and break every yoke,
to share your bread with the hungry,
and shelter the homeless poor,

to clothe the man you see to be naked
and not turn from your own kin?
Then will the light shine like the dawn
and your wound be quickly healed over.

Your integrity will go before you
and the glory of Yahweh behind you.
Cry, and Yahweh will answer;
call, and he will say, "I am here."

If you do away with the yoke,
the clenched fist, the wicked word,
if you give your bread to the hungry,
and relief to the oppressed,

your light will rise in the darkness,
and your shadows become like noon.
Yahweh will always guide you,
giving you relief in desert places.

He will give strength to your bones
and you shall be like a watered garden,
like a spring of water
whose waters never run dry.

You will rebuild the ancient ruins,
build up on the old foundations. (58:6–12)

Lord, send your Spirit of love upon us so that we may find
the courage to leave our closets and become creative agents of
your love. Amen.

Part Two

Intimacy with God

Introduction: Feeling the Presence of God

I have a vivid memory of the shock I experienced when, as a novice in the Society of Jesus, I first read Saint Ignatius Loyola's *Spiritual Exercises*. In a discussion of morning prayer, Saint Ignatius recommends preparing subjects for meditation the night before. However, as you begin prayer in the morning, Ignatius writes, you should pause for a moment before you begin to meditate in order to recall that you are in the presence of God, and, if God gives you the grace to *feel* that presence, then you may rest in that feeling and forget about reflecting further on the subjects you prepared.

Ignatius's point is that sometimes God in her graciousness gives us right away what we are seeking: a felt presence and a communion of love. Thus, to turn our attention away from that immediate experience to other subjects of meditation is in some way to ignore God. In a way it is like watching television or reading the newspaper when your lover would like to spend some time talking with you.

What came as a shock to me was the fact that, although I was consciously spending that early morning hour in prayer, I had a great resistance to feeling the presence of God. The lid slid back for a second on a cauldron of seething emotions—feelings of anger, fear, and guilt—of which I was not fully conscious. It began to dawn on me that, although God may have wanted to have an intimate, direct, personal relationship with me, in various ways I had been placing obstacles in the way of that intimacy. The very idea of that intimate presence was provoking intense emotional reactions in me of which I was not fully aware.

Experts in the field of spiritual direction define this practice as "the help given by one Christian to another which enables that person to pay attention to God's personal communication to her or him, to respond to this personally communicating God, to grow in intimacy with God, and to live out the consequences of that relationship."[1] The authors point out that the focus of this form of guidance is on experience, and this experience is not an isolated event but rather an expression of the ongoing personal relationship God has established with each one of us.

Certainly those of us who grew up as lesbian or gay Christians could have used a skilled, nonhomophobic spiritual director. But few of us, if any, had that privilege. In part 2 of this book I will deal with the three principal emotions that prevent intimacy with God: anger, fear, and guilt. I will also examine the special issues that arise for gay and lesbian people because of these feelings.

Before beginning this discussion I would like to repeat a fundamental principle: Whatever is good psychology is good theology, and vice versa. If living out our understanding of the Scriptures and God's law leads to our human destruction, if in attempting to live that life we become neurotic, depressed, addicted to drugs or alcohol, irritable, and unhappy, then something is wrong with our theological understanding, and something is especially wrong in our personal relationship with God.

The great heresy of pathological religion is that we can only give glory to God when we are frustrated, unhappy, or suffering. This misconception led to Marx's famous critique of religion: Whatever glorifies God denies the human. Therefore, whatever will build the human must be based on a denial of God.

The exact opposite of Marx's understanding of Christianity can be found in the creation spirituality of Meister Eckhardt. That spirituality works on the principle that we are called on by God to "choose life." The first principle of Christian living is that we are to enjoy life in a spirit of gratitude to God for all the good gifts of life, and we are to strive to share that enjoyment with as many others as possible. Our prayer should be: Thank you, God, for these thy gifts; grant them also to all those in need.

To be able to choose life, we must deal with the major obstacles to intimacy. In Genesis, God is recorded as saying: "It is not good that the man should be alone. I will make him a helpmate" (2:18). My hope is that the following chapters will help all my lesbian and gay sisters and brothers to identify and eliminate the obstacles to their intimacy with each other and with God.

5

Dealing with Anger

I set before you life or death, blessing or curse. Choose life, then. . . .
Deuteronomy 30:19

The emotion of anger, along with its relation to our spiritual life and our life of intimacy with each other and with God, is often seriously misunderstood. One of the greatest challenges that has always faced the lesbian and gay community has been how to deal creatively and productively with all the anger that necessarily results from our frequent alienation from family, church, and society. A new and sometimes overwhelming dimension has been added to that anger because of the AIDS epidemic.

Some of the anger about AIDS has been confused and unfocused, which has made dealing with it more difficult. Should the person with AIDS be angry at the person who exposed him, if he knows who that person is? Should we be angry with ourselves because of the behavior that actually or potentially exposed us to AIDS, or should we be angry for coming out of the closet in the first place? Should we be angry at the gay community for adopting a life-style that permitted the spread of the disease? Should we be angry at the medical profession for failing to treat the disease, or the government for inadequate funding of research and education? Should we be angry at the Church and society for refusing us the right to a monogamous life-style protected by the law? Or should we be angry with God, who seems to be playing into the hands of our enemies by allowing a deadly disease to be associated with our way of life?

Because of this difficulty in focusing our anger, it is easy for that anger to erupt in neurotic, self-destructive ways. Depression, for example, can be a form of "swallowed" anger, anger that we turn in on ourselves because we don't see any way to express it creatively. We can, however, achieve a better understanding of the role that anger plays in our lives, and a better understanding of how to deal with anger in a healthy and constructive way, especially that most difficult form of anger—anger at God.

During the Middle Ages in a mountainous region of France, victims of hypothyroidism were called cretins because they were always restrained, taciturn, dull, and unemotional. Surprisingly, the word *cretin* meant Christian, because in the popular mind these unfortunate, sick people epitomized the kind of unemotional saintliness that the people confused with true Christian behavior. We, too, are frequently brought up to feel that good Christians should never be angry or be hostile toward anyone. Consequently, even to feel anger seems to be sinful. We are therefore taught to repress and deny all angry feelings.

The primary mechanism of denial that most of us instinctively use, adults as well as children, is what I term the "Keeping-Mother-Good" syndrome. (This syndrome also applies to father insofar as he plays an active role in childrearing.) The child is absolutely dependent on the goodness and love of the parenting figure. If mother is not good and loving, then the infant experiences anger and frustration. However, the child becomes fearful that this anger will drive the mother away. For the child, to lose mother would be like losing life itself. Thus the child will strive instinctively to deny and suppress any feelings of anger. The best way children have of doing this is to lower their self-image and direct their anger toward themselves: "I must have been very bad to make mother so angry at me." Once a child has learned this mechanism for dealing with anger, there is a tendency to handle anger in this way for the rest of his or her life. When in later life such a person is treated badly, he or she does not get angry at the mistreating person, but directs the anger inward toward him- or herself.

We have all heard of cases in which a drug-addicted mother has amused herself by burning her child with her cigarette.

When someone asks the child what kind of parent could do such a thing, the child will almost inevitably respond: "My mother is good. She would never have done this if I hadn't been so bad." In these extreme circumstances, the mechanism for keeping mother good is a healthy psychological solution because it allows the child to stay in touch with reality and preserve the illusion that he or she has some control. The only other choice frequently is psychotic breakdown. The problem arises, however, when this unconscious mechanism is continued into adulthood where it precludes other, healthier responses. Similar mechanisms for repressing anger are common among children of alcoholic parents.

This mechanism is frequently reinforced by the religious instruction the child receives. Many of us were brought up to believe that all anger is sinful, and we received mixed messages from Scripture. Passages such as "anyone who is angry with his brother will answer for it before the court" (Mt. 5:22) and "never have grudges against others, or lose your temper, or raise your voice to anybody" (Ep. 4:31) seem to imply that all anger is evil. On the other hand, we cherish the image of an angry Jesus, whip in hand, driving the moneychangers out of the temple and overturning the tables, or, again, calling his enemies "whitewashed tombs that look handsome on the outside, but inside are full of dead men's bones" (Mt. 23:27). If Jesus knew anger, then anger cannot simply be equated with sin. All the great prophets, too, were angry men and women who channelled their anger into a passionate search for justice.

Since we develop our ideas and feelings about anger and our unconscious habits of dealing with it as children, we may have difficulty comprehending the subtle difference between being angry at someone and hating that person. We have trouble fathoming what Saint Paul meant when he wrote: "Even if you are angry, you must not sin: never let the sun set on your anger or else you will give the devil a foothold" (Ep. 4:26–27). At least Paul does not identify anger with sin in this passage. He does however, advise us to deal with our anger and let go of it, lest it lead to sinful hatred and hostility. Herein lies one of the great secrets of anger: anger that is experienced as powerful is easily dealt with, but anger that is experienced as powerless can easily turn into real hatred.

A tragic example of this can be found in those persons with AIDS who will not refrain from sexual encounters that they know can endanger the lives of their sexual partners. "Somebody gave it to me," one declared angrily, "so I'm going to give it to somebody else!"

Contemporary psychology has taught us the importance of learning to consciously accept all our emotions as natural and inevitable, even when they are negative. We must learn to be grateful for all our feelings and learn to accept and cope with them deliberately in positive and constructive ways, rather than to repress them into the unconscious where they can quickly be transformed into mental or physical illness. Unexpressed anger produces stress in the system, which, if prolonged, leads to high blood pressure, heart attacks, peptic ulcers, colitis, strokes, and even immune deficiency. Doctors tell us that if we can learn to deal with our anger successfully we can add at least twenty years to our life. "Choose life!"

Anger is an emotion we all experience to some degree every day of our lives. It is a natural, inevitable response to frustration or deprivation. Just as pain follows a physical wound, anger occurs when we feel we are being dealt with unjustly. Anger can be defined as *psychic pain*. Experts have shown that in neurotic family structures, no one is allowed to feel and express anger, whereas in healthy families anger is positively appreciated. Children are encouraged to feel and express their anger, and when they express it they are listened to. It is safe to assume that if someone is angry, they are hurting. Consequently, one does the best one can to listen and respond. The result is that children who grow up in such a family are free to feel and express their anger. They feel powerful in their anger. Having expressed their anger and received satisfactory results, they can then let go of it.

The importance of this psychological insight for our emotional and spiritual life is that there can be no real intimacy without the ability to deal honestly and openly with anger. As soon as one begins to grow close to someone and develop a mutual intimacy, one will necessarily feel anger frequently and strongly. I fact, I sometimes believe that we really only get angry in a passionate way with those we love. Getting in touch with our anger at someone we love and expressing it renders us vulnerable. It takes a lot of courage, and it is a profound act of trust and love.

We cannot repress and deny that anger without repressing and denying *all* feelings, including feelings of tenderness and love. If we did so, we would have to learn to live in our heads, dealing with everything with a cold intellect instead of a warm heart. Feelings are like a bowl of spaghetti: you can never get only one strand—they all come together. Similarly, you can never select out just one feeling to deal with or repress. You must deal with all your feelings, including anger, or repress them all.

Usually, the first sign that repressed anger is building up between a couple is a drop-off in their sex life. Repressed anger is the best anti-aphrodisiac one can find. Many couples find that, after a good fight in which they are both able to communicate their pent-up anger, the sexual union that follows is better than ever. Sadly, it is also the case that many couples, after years of living together, no longer have a sex life because there is too much suppressed anger between them.

If anger between couples is not dealt with in a conscious, healthy way, it will leak out in pathological and destructive ways. Passive aggressive behavior—being habitually late, being sarcastic, engaging in verbal abuse, always putting one's partner down—is usually disguised anger. Anger can also get displaced onto "innocent bystanders," because that way it seems less threatening. One's friends, co-workers, the passengers on the morning subway or bus, or other drivers on the highway can thus become the unwitting victims of all the displaced rage one feels toward one's partner.

If we can't get in touch with our anger, or if we don't feel we have the freedom and the trust to share it, it will quickly grow into a brick wall, cutting us off from others. Eventually, the pain that our partner's presence causes us because of the repressed anger we feel outweighs any pleasure we might experience, and the relationship disintegrates. However, if we can risk sharing our anger and our partner can hear it and respond to it in such a way that we feel free to let go of it, then the bonds of trust and love and intimacy grow deeper and more secure and the joy of intimate sharing increases. But to reach this point, we must take a chance and risk being vulnerable to our partner by openly sharing any feelings of anger. Among the gay and lesbian couples that I have counseled, my experience has been that if the people involved give each other permission to communicate anger, and if they can respond nondefensively, then that relationship has a good chance of surviving.

The key point I would like to make here is that our spiritual life is an effort to develop an intimacy with God, an intimate sense of God's presence. Just as anger is a natural and inevitable part of our life of intimacy with a fellow human being, it is also a natural and inevitable part of our life of intimacy with God. If we turn to God in prayer and feel we are not heard and there is no answer, we feel frustrated and angry. Normally we repress and deny that anger. We keep God good by turning the anger onto ourselves. We ask, "What right do I have to expect God to listen to my prayers?"

Gradually, a wall gets built up in our unconscious until we find it intolerable to be in the presence of God, intolerable because we feel threatened if we try to get in touch with our anger. So we quit praying; we give up on going to church. Our spiritual life dries up. One of my clients was so traumatized by the homophobia of the southern Baptist church of his childhood, that the only way he could relate to God peacefully and without traumatic anger was by converting to Judaism.

I believe there is a particular danger here for lesbian women and gay men, especially in this time of AIDS. In a recent report by the First International Lesbian/Gay Health Conference, Pat Norman, coordinator of Lesbian and Gay Health Services for the city of San Francisco, was reported as saying "self-hatred has supported our continued feelings of worthlessness and inadequacy and these feelings have spurred alcoholism, drug abuse and suicide."[1] In a workshop at the same conference, John E. Ryan spoke of the male homosexual's shame, self-contempt, and rage: "the most important and necessary change that psychotherapists can achieve in working with homosexual men is to alleviate the negative self-beliefs, self-feelings and self-attitudes that are internalized, taken in as part of the self."[2]

For many Christians and especially for Catholic gays, a large part of that crippling self-hatred has its source in their effort to keep Mother Church good. The church has a long history of homophobia. John Boswell in his brilliant book *Christianity, Social Tolerance, and Homosexuality*[3] seriously disputes the belief that the church's doctrinal and pastoral attitude toward homosexuality has always had the same homophobic virulence as it has had in recent centuries. The church has read homophobic meanings into scriptural passages where they are not to be found; its sexual ethics is based on a homophobic premise; and its pastoral practice is seriously destructive of the mental health and well being of hundreds of thousands of humans.

The recent actions of the Roman Catholic Church have intensified the virulence of its homophobia. For example, the Halloween pastoral letter of 1986 to all the bishops of the world repeats the homophobic interpretations of Scripture and human nature and reaffirms the homophobia of tradition. But even beyond that, the letter reveals a mean and cruel spirit that is difficult to associate with a Christian community. It hints that gay people who have worked for the liberation of their gay and lesbian brothers and sisters may be responsible for the AIDS crisis. It calls on all the bishops of the world to defeat any effort to achieve gay civil rights on the grounds that "sin has no right." And it even suggests that the victims of anti-gay violence deserve what they get when they seek "unthinkable rights." Finally, the letter calls for the expulsion from church property of all gay groups that seek to integrate healthy gay identity with religious faith.

Understandably, there is a legitimate rage in the gay community against the human and fallible church. I would like to explore some of the healthy and some of the pathological ways of dealing with that rage. One pathological response is to try to keep Mother Church good. To do so, one must conform to the church's homophobic teaching, see oneself as "intrinsically disordered," and see one's desire for sexual expression as a "tendency to evil." One must then repress all sexual feelings (and with them, all other feelings). Any person who does this necessarily hates an essential part of him- or herself, and this self-hatred frequently spills over in a paranoid hatred of all homosexuals. It is these self-hating gays within the church's power structure who frequently become our worst persecutors.

The Catholic Church would prefer to keep gay people isolated from one another, as it did in the past. But now that there are openly gay religious groups, the church for the first time has allowed a group to exist called Courage. The purpose of the group is to help gay individuals conform to church teaching by repressing their sexual needs and living lives of enforced celibacy. This group, in my opinion, serves a useful purpose only for those individuals whose sexual orientation is so egodystonic that, if they acted on their feelings, they would be threatened with emotional breakdown. However, the very basis of this group is pathological self-hatred. If there is any possibility of escaping that self-hatred without risking worse evil, then I believe the individual is morally obliged to do so.

Other churches have adopted a policy of accepting gay members, but their homophobia is expressed in more subtle ways, such as refusing ordination to a gay candidate unless that candidate promises to live a celibate life.

For many gay people, dealing with the church is like dealing with parents. Even if we seriously disagree with them and see what they have done to us as truly destructive, we still love them and are grateful for what they have done for us and given us. But that love does not negate the fact that we have been wounded by them, and as long as we remain wounded, there is unavoidable anger. The only healthy way to let go of that anger is to heal the wounds of self-hatred and self-rejection and strive to achieve an attitude of positive self-acceptance.

Many gay Christians have healed the wounds inflicted on them by the church; they have learned to accept and live out their gayness in good conscience. These people frequently feel strong enough to remain in the church and participate in its sacramental life and in all its aspects that are relatively unpolluted by homophobia, while praying and doing whatever they can to raise the church's consciousness on the issue of homosexuality. Over the past year, a number of courageous gay Catholics have gone every first Sunday of the month to Saint Patrick's Cathedral where, during the cardinal's sermon, they stand in silent protest against the homophobia of the church. (On December 6, 1987, church authorities called in the police and had those who were standing arrested and placed under criminal charges that could result in a year in prison.)

Many others, however, are so wounded by the homophobia of the human church that they need to withdraw for a time and seek out an accepting community such as the Metropolitan Community Church (half of whose members are exiled Catholics) or other religious communities in which they can heal their wounds, such as the Unitarian Universalist church, where they are accepted and their relationships can be celebrated.

Unfortunately, there are large numbers who cannot separate off their membership in the human church from their faith in God and their personal spiritual relationship with God. These people see only two choices: either to remain in their church at the price of hating themselves and repressing their homosexuality as evil, or to accept themselves as homosexual and then denying or repressing their religious beliefs. As a result, they are tempted to throw out all religious faith and live impoverished lives. My hope in these pages is to describe a third alternative: one that involves confronting the church while deepening one's faith.

Beyond the issue of anger at the church, for many gay people there is also the issue of anger at God. Since we do not usually choose our sexual orientation, we experience it as a given, an objective fact that is part of God's creation. Insofar as our experience of our sexual orientation is negative, as long as we see it as sinful, sick, or evil, we experience a deep crisis in our relationship with God and real anger at God. Only a sadistic God would create millions of humans as gay with no choice in the matter and no hope of changing and then deny them the right to express their gayness in a loving relationship for the rest of their lives under threat of eternal damnation.

AIDS adds a new dimension to that anger with God. If we accept the blasphemous proposition that AIDS is God's punishment for being gay, then we may justly feel rage against the sadistic God who creates humans gay and then punishes them with a deadly disease for being what they were created.

Once again, the only way to forgive someone we see as having wounded us is to heal the wound. We gay people must risk believing that God is not homophobic even though the human church is. We must learn to accept our gayness as a gift from God and live it out joyfully in a way that is compatible with God's law. In that process of self-acceptance and in our new awareness of God's love for us, we can then let go of our anger.

At the heart of all gay spiritual life is a process of mourning and accepting our status as exiles in this world. That mourning process is doubly difficult for anyone who has AIDS. Every healthy mourning process necessarily involves a period of intense anger which must be dealt with. Many gay people, however, find it almost impossible to get in touch with their anger at God. One does not dare get in touch with anger if the God one is serving is a God of fear. If good parents know how to accept and respond to the anger of their children, then surely God, who shared our human nature in Jesus and had a first-hand experience of human anger, knows how to accept and respond to our human anger. In fact, Jesus gave us a model of how to express and deal with anger in the parable of the prodigal son (Lk. 15:11–32).

The prodigal son returns home after squandering his inheritance on self-indulgent pleasures. The elder son, who remained at home and worked faithfully on the family farm, returns home from a day in the fields and finds a celebration in full swing. He calls a servant to find out what is going on, and is enraged at the injustice of it all. He says to his father, "You never offered me so much as a kid for me to celebrate with my friends" (Lk. 15:29), and refuses to go in and join the celebration. (The equivalent action in our own lives would be our refusal to go to church while we are angry and demand that God come out and meet us on our own terms.) The father, however, respects his eldest son's anger and goes out to speak with him. He recognizes that his son deserves a hearing and an explanation. He also assures his son that he will be dealt with justly, and tells him, "Everything I have is yours." Although the parable doesn't explicitly say so, I think we can assume that the elder son, because his anger was respected and listened to and because he could feel that his anger had some effect, was able to let go of his anger and join the celebration.

If we feel that our spiritual life is drying up, if we cannot stand to go to church, then we must ask ourselves whether we are angry with God. We must learn how to feel that anger and not deny it. We must learn to trust God enough to bring that anger into our prayers and share it with God. Remember that sharing anger is an act of love. We must demand that God let us know that our anger has been heard. If we can do this, we will be surprised at the warmth, closeness, and intimacy we will experience with God.

Apart from discovering my own gayness, the most traumatic event of my life was the death of my mother when I was three years old. The only conscious memory I have of her is an image of me lying in a crib in my father's bedroom on a sunny summer morning and hearing my mother's frightened voice saying, "What will happen to my babies?" as medics carried her downstairs on her final trip to the hospital. These were the last words I ever heard my mother speak. Whatever anger I felt at God I repressed as a child, and I grew up with a vague feeling that because I had been a bad child I was somehow responsible for the death of my mother. Needless to say, I grew up with a God I feared. It was not until I reached late adulthood that I was able, with the help of a good therapist, to get in touch with my anger at God. Once I had successfully done so, I had a tendency to return in prayer to that old wound and the anger accompanying it. Last Christmas season, feeling once again like a "motherless child," I slipped into Saint Jean Baptist Church on the east side of New York and knelt in prayer before the altar of the Virgin, which has a beautiful statue of Mary with her child Jesus.

As I was praying I felt anger swell up inside me, and almost in tears of rage I heard myself praying: "This is a fine situation. Jesus, you claimed to be like all the rest of us in all things but sin. That's not true. First of all, you chose for yourself a sinless mother capable of perfect love. No other human had that advantage. Then you took away my mother while I was still a baby! Then you chose for yourself a saint as a perfect father, Joseph, who taught you the skills of carpentry. My father was a distant, quiet man with whom I cannot remember ever having a conversation about feelings. Finally, at your baptism God the Father shouted from heaven: 'This is my beloved son in whom I am well pleased.'" I, on the other hand, had lived most of my life feeling that, because of my gayness, I was profoundly displeasing to God. I remember summing up my prayer with the words: "With all those privileges, anyone could stand to undergo a little crucifixion!"

As I knelt there, my eyes filled with tears. I quietly heard another voice within me saying: Why are you so filled with self-pity? And why are you so ungrateful? Twenty-two years ago, I sent a friend into your life who has given you more mothering than any human has a right to. Every night he has dinner on the table when you finish with your last client. He worries about you day and night; he continually prays for you, supports you, and misses you when you are away; he makes sure you have clean underwear and that your hair is combed. He holds you and comforts you when you are frightened or sick. He does you the honor of being angry at you when you do something thoughtless or hurtful. I have more than made up to you for the loss you suffered as a child.

As these thoughts passed through my spirit, I was filled with shame and remorse at my lack of gratitude. I realized that for twenty-two years I had been holding on to an old grudge and had failed to recognize the gift God had given me. Through the grace of God, I was able to take one more step in letting go of my god of fear and feel a deeper intimacy than ever before with my God of love. I was able to forgive God.

Almighty God, you have promised to remain forever with those who do what is just and right. Help us lesbian women and gay men to live in your presence. Help us to deal in a healthy way with the anger that threatens to cut us off from that presence. Please remember that if we are angry with you, it is because we love you. Amen.

Liberation from Fear

Do not be afraid.

Luke 2:10

Fear permeates the human community today, but it is so all-pervasive and so repressed that for the most part we live unaware of it. There are the ordinary fears of life common to all humans: fear of alienation and loneliness; fear of sickness, pain, and death; fear of poverty and insecurity; and fear of rejection both human and divine. As Henri Nouwen puts it in his book *Lifesigns,* "We are fearful people. . . . It often seems that fear has invaded every part of our being to such a degree that we no longer know what a life without fear feels like."[1]

There never is a moment that is totally free from fear. In fact, fear has so deeply penetrated our psyches that it controls most of our decisions, choices, and actions. Much of the fear we live with has been repressed into the unconscious, and it is frequently what lies behind our anger and rage. Fear can drive us into depression and despair.

Darkness is the great biblical symbol for a life permeated by fear. Fear surrounds us like darkness, and makes us feel that we are perilously close to death and destruction. Fear of a nuclear holocaust has so permeated the lives of many of our young people that they have lost any hope for the future. Many ask whether it is fair to bring a baby into a world threatened by nuclear warfare. Fear can become so intolerable that even suicide becomes an acceptable way to escape it. As Nouwen remarks, "In fact, most of us people of the twentieth century live in the house of fear most of the time."[2]

Jim Forrest, in a wonderful article on the meaning of Christmas entitled "Be Not Afraid,"[3] recounts an old rabbinical story about the meaning of the night. The rabbi asks one of his students, "When can one know that the night has ended and the day has begun?" "Is it," one student suggests, "that moment when you can tell the difference between a sheep and a dog?" "No," says the rabbi, "that isn't it." "Is it," asks another, "when you can see the difference between a fig tree and an olive tree?" "Not that either," says the rabbi. "Rather," he says, "it is that moment when you can look at a face never seen before and recognize the stranger as a brother or sister. Until that moment, no matter how bright the day, it is still the night."

Most of us, Forrest adds, live in that night most of our lives. We are trained to accept that night by our families, schools, country, and often by the church itself. We are carefully schooled not to recognize brothers or sisters but rather to see friends or enemies, us versus them. We are trained to see labels that allow us to dehumanize and dominate others: chauvinistic labels like Jap or geek; racist labels like kike or nigger; sexist labels like dyke or queer. Our own fear, anger, and distrust become a paranoid hatred of anything or anyone different.

Why are we so afraid? The answer, according to Nouwen, can be found in the relation of fear to power: "I began to see the simple fact that those I fear have a great power over me. Those who could make me afraid could also make me do what they wanted me to do."[4] In order to be liberated from the control of fear, we must first bring into full consciousness this close connection between our fear and the power that others have over us.

Most authority tries to control us by means of fear. For example, Alice Miller, in her book *For Your Own Good: Hidden Cruelty in Child-Rearing and the Roots of Violence,*[5] sees the whole history of pedagogy as based on the idea that the way to produce obedient children is to terrorize them. The unacknowledged premise of this system is that it is better to have an obedient child than to have that child's love. Many schools try to educate their pupils through fear of punishment or of failure. Most employers use the fear of being fired or of losing a raise or promotion to control their employees. Many churches make use of a god of fear to control their members. One has only to tune in to any television evangelist to hear how frequently they make skillful use of fear to manipulate and control their audience. The quickest route to wealth in America today is to arouse fear in the public and then claim you have a way to alleviate that fear.

There are countless forms of fear deliberately cultivated by those who want to control and manipulate us: fears based on racism and sexism, fears of nuclear warfare, fears of a communist takeover. Those who stir up these fears control us by making us think that our fears will come true unless we are compliant. If we acquiesce to that control, we join forces with the agents of fear and become "determined guardians of the night."

Gays and lesbians need to develop a conscious awareness of the destructive role of fear in their community. Our greatest enemy is not some outside opponent—it is the fear within us. First of all there are the fears we share with all humanity. But there are also fears that are unique to us as gay people. Because of our gayness, we may be subject to fears that lead to staying in the closet, self-denial, self-rejection, self-hatred, and finally even fleeing from the presence of God. We frequently give in to our own form of homophobic fear that crushes out all love for our lesbian sisters and gay brothers. Instead of seeing the glory of God in our being fully alive as lesbians and gay men, we sometimes believe that God's glory lies in our self-rejection and self-persecution, as well as in the rejection and persecution of our brothers and sisters. But as terrifying as all these fears are, there is a fear pervading American society today, especially in the gay community, that outdoes all others in its destructiveness: it is a disease of the spirit based on a fear of AIDS, which some in the gay community have referred to as FRAIDS. After centuries of oppression and alienation, lesbians and gay men in the last twenty years have won through to an extraordinary degree of healthy self-acceptance and political freedom. The AIDS crisis threatens to wipe out all these gains by creating such an atmosphere of hysteria and fear that it could drive gay people back into the closet.

The fear that AIDS has provoked among gay people is so profound that it is difficult to be fully conscious of all its dimensions. Chris Glaser, in his article "AIDS and the A-Bomb Disease: Facing a Special Death,"[6] turned to Robert Jay Lifton's analysis[7] of the experience of the survivors of the bombing of Hiroshima for a basis of comparison with the gay person's experience of AIDS.

For example, both Hiroshima survivors and gay people with AIDS experience a permanent encounter with death. The average age of those who die from AIDS is thirty-six. Gay people have not only seen the deaths of friends, acquaintances, and strangers in ever-increasing numbers, they may also feel that their whole world is dying. The gay community, built with blood, sweat, and tears over the past eighteen years since the Stonewall uprising, seems to be threatened with extinction.

One of my clients wrote a short story about three elderly people taking part in their last parade up Fifth Avenue on Gay Pride Day in the year 2000. They are the only survivors of the gay liberation movement of the seventies, nostalgically remembering the hundreds of thousands who marched twenty years before but who are now all dead as a result of AIDS or have been driven back into the closet by fear.

A second similarity between the survivors of Hiroshima and gay people is the threat of invisible contamination. Because of the intense radiation they were exposed to, those who survived the atomic bomb may be struck down at any moment. Since the incubation period for AIDS can be as long as ten years or more, we members of the gay community must also live with a similar fear of invisible contamination that can strike at any moment.

The third parallel is the fact that, for Hiroshima survivors, any symptoms of illness—a cold, fatigue, flu, or fever—became associated with the atomic bomb and its images of death. So, too, if we in the gay community feel fatigue or come down with any ailment, our thoughts and anxieties immediately turn to AIDS and the fear of death. The resulting stress makes us even more vulnerable to disease.

We may also experience stress because of the fears of those who love us. Parents are fearful for their sons; the danger of disease seems always present. Bad news could come at any moment. The father of one of my clients told me that having a gay son living in New York City provoked even greater fear and anxiety in him than when his older son was serving in Vietnam.

Two other fears associated with AIDS anxiety should also be mentioned. The first is the fear of all the difficulties of a protracted, debilitating disease: loss of income; frequent, painful hospital stays; and the deprivation of emotional nourishment as fearful friends hesitate to visit, touch, or embrace us. The second is an increasing fear of intimacy, since sexual intimacy is the primary way to communicate the HIV virus. To have death associated with intimacy further inhibits gay men who have already been socialized to avoid intimacy.

I will deal specifically with the fear of death in chapters 17, 18, and 19. At this point I want to explore what Jesus had to say about fear and what spiritual resources we can bring to bear in our struggle to liberate ourselves from the control of fear.

Our Spiritual Life and Liberation from Fear

"Do not be afraid." Liberation from fear is a key element of our salvation. It is also a central message of the New Testament. God sent Jesus to liberate us from the dominion of fear, which is the dominion and the power of the evil one. We have a tendency to sentimentalize Christmas. We forget that Jesus was born into a militarized society under Roman occupation, where anyone who stood up for their rights quickly found their way to the torturers and death on a cross. The day after Christmas we commemorate the memory of Stephen, the first Christian martyr, who was stoned to death. Two days after Christmas we remember the Holy Innocents—all those children who were hacked to death because of Herod's paranoid fear that his power might be threatened by the infant Jesus.

Herod is alive and well in our world. He is alive in those responsible for institutionalized violence. Herod issued the orders and his soldiers carried them out. Nouwen tells the story of a Guatemalan Indian forcibly taken from his family and inducted into the army. He was forced to torture and kill his fellow Indians, under threat of the same fate if he refused. When he finally was allowed to visit his family again, his father refused to let him enter his house. He was told that he could greet his mother but would then have to move on because "you carry death with you."[8]

Although there are innumerable kinds of destructive fear, we should bear in mind that not all fear is unhealthy. One healthy kind is the "fear of God" frequently recommended in the Bible, which refers to the profound awe we feel at the power and majesty of God as ruler of the universe. The poet Rainer Maria

Rilke, thinking of that kind of awe, wrote, "Beauty is naught but the beginning of terror." This same kind of awe lay behind the words of God to Moses on Mount Sinai when God said, "You cannot see my face . . . for a man cannot see me and live" (Ex. 33:20).

There is another healthy form of fear: the fear of injuring the one we love. This fear is a corollary to our experience of being loved. Children develop a healthy fear of hurting the parents who love them. So too, an adult who has developed an intimacy with God fears to do anything that would diminish that intimacy.

The fear that we should seek to be liberated from is that kind of paranoid fear that impoverishes our conscience and cripples our response to those around us, numbing us to their needs because of anxiety about our own needs, blinding us in such a way that we fail to recognize those around us as our brothers and sisters. We have recently seen many examples of this paranoid fear leading to cruel and destructive treatment of people with AIDS, for instance, the expulsion of children with AIDS from their schools, or a neighborhood refusing to allow a residence for homeless people with AIDS to be opened. Fear of this sort deadens the soul and diminishes our capacity for awe and wonder, and drives us back into the closet. This kind of pathological fear is Satan's primary weapon; it is the source of the nuclear arms race and of the threat of total destruction for humanity and our planet. This is the fear from which Jesus sought to liberate us.

Before the coming of our Savior the whole world was under the dominion of fear. Certainly the pagan gods ruled their superstitious subjects through fear. Those worshipers of Baal who brought their firstborn children and threw them into the fire before the idol as a sacrifice did so out of fear. They believed that, if they did not sacrifice their children, their god would punish them with famine, barrenness, pestilence, and war. Recently archeologists discovered a mass graveyard in the city of Carthage filled with thousands of urns containing the ashes of children who had been offered as human sacrifices to the god of that city.

In the Christmas story, we are told that shepherds were out in the fields keeping watch over their flocks. An angel appears to them, and they are filled with fear. The angel says to them, "Be not afraid." These are some of the most important and most ignored words in the Bible. It is a message spoken to us over and

over again. When God says these words to us, they are more than
just a pious wish; they are sacramental words that produce the
effect they ask for. "The angel said '. . . I bring you news of great
joy, a joy to be shared by the whole people. Today in the town of
David, a savior has been born to you; he is Christ the Lord'" (Lk.
2:10–11). We are told that the shepherds courageously hurried to
Bethlehem and, after seeing Jesus with his mother, returned
"glorifying and praising God for all they had heard and seen"
(Lk. 2:20).

The shepherds were not the only ones to receive the message
of liberation from fear. The angel said the same thing to Mary
when her pregnancy began: "Mary, do not be afraid; you have
won God's favor" (Lk. 1:30). Mary's brave statement, "let what
you have said be done to me" (Lk. 1:38), is followed by her
courageous prayer, the Magnificat: "My soul proclaims the
greatness of the Lord and my spirit exults in God my savior"
(Lk. 1:46–47).

Similar words were spoken to Joseph when he was hesitant
to marry a woman who had become pregnant before the wedding: "Joseph . . . do not be afraid to take Mary home as your
wife, because she has conceived what is in her by the Holy
Spirit" (Mt. 2:20), and again when the angel told Zechariah, "do
not be afraid, your prayer has been heard. Your wife Elizabeth is
to bear you a son and you must name him John" (Lk. 1:13).
Zechariah's prophecy at the birth of John contains these words:
"Blessed be the Lord, the God of Israel, for he has visited his
people . . . and remembers his holy covenant, the oath . . . that
he would grant us, free from fear, to be delivered from the hands
of our enemies, to serve him in holiness and virtue . . . you will
go before the Lord . . . to give light to those who live in darkness
and the shadow of death, and to guide our feet into the way of
peace" (Lk. 2:68–79).

The message of liberation from fear permeates the Gospels.
To demonstrate how central this theme was to Jesus' message, I
would like to draw together here every major instance in Scripture where Jesus sought to free his disciples from the dominion
of fear. In chapter 10 of Matthew, he tells them, "When they
hand you over, do not worry about how to speak or what to say;
what you are to say will be given to you when the time comes"
(v. 19). And again he tells them, "Do not be afraid of them therefore" (v. 26). On frequent occasions, Jesus warned his disciples

not to let their lives be ruled by anxiety but to trust the Lord. For example, in chapter 12 of Luke Jesus tells them, "That is why I am telling you not to worry about your life and what you are to eat, nor about your body and how you are to clothe it." And again, "You men of little faith! But you, you must not set your hearts on things to eat and things to drink, nor must you worry. . . . No; set your heart on [God's] kingdom, and these other things will be given to you as well. There is no need to be afraid, little flock, for it has pleased your Father to give you the kingdom" (vv. 22–33).

Another striking episode is the famous scene when Jesus came to his disciples, walking on the water, when their boat was caught in a storm. When the disciples saw him thus, we are told, they were terrified, and thought they were seeing a ghost. "But at once Jesus called out to them saying, 'Courage! It is I! Do not be afraid.'" Peter then got out of the boat and began to walk on the water toward Jesus. As long as Peter kept his attention firmly fixed on Jesus, he was all right. But the text tells us that he became distracted by the fierce wind, and as his attention wavered he became afraid and began to sink. He then called out to Jesus, "Lord! Save me!" Jesus reached out and saved him, but rebuked him with the words, "Man of little faith . . . why did you doubt?" (Mt. 14:22–33).

Another instance of a storm at sea is mentioned in Mark 4:35–41. The disciples and Jesus were in a boat that was threatened by huge waves, but Jesus was sleeping peacefully on a cushion in the stern. The disciples woke him with a rebuke: "Master, do you not care? We are going down!" Jesus calmed the sea and said to them, "Why are you so frightened? How is it that you have no faith?"

It was fear that led Peter to deny Christ three times in the courtyard of the high priest. But his three declarations of love for Jesus made up for those failures and restored Peter to leadership in the community of love (Jn. 21:15–19).

The Transfiguration (Mt. 17:1–8) provided another occasion where Jesus attempted to teach his disciples freedom from fear. (It is interesting to note that the three apostles whom Jesus brought with him to see his glory—Peter, James, and John—were the same three who would be asked to be with him in his moment of agony in the garden of Gethsemane—an example of how God never asks anything of us without offering the grace to deal with it.) Again, when the disciples fell to the ground in fear, Jesus came and touched them reassuringly and said, "Stand up . . . do not be afraid" (Mt. 17:8).

Certainly the climax of Jesus' efforts to liberate his disciples from fear occurred after the Resurrection. At the Last Supper, Jesus promises a special gift of peace: "Peace I bequeath to you, my own peace I give to you. . . . Do not let your hearts be troubled or afraid" (Jn. 14:27). Following Jesus' passion and death, we are told that the disciples stayed hidden in the upper room out of fear. The first words Jesus speaks to them when he appears are a message of peace and reassurance: "Why are you so agitated and why are these doubts rising in your hearts? Look at my hands and my feet; yes, it is I indeed. Touch me and see for yourselves; a ghost has no flesh and bones as you can see I have" (Lk. 24:38–39).

What seems to have been the decisive event in the disciples' liberation from fear was the descent upon them of the Holy Spirit. Following that event, they came out of the upper room and fearlessly proclaimed the message of Christ's salvation. Even when they were imprisoned and beaten, we are told that "they left the presence of the Sanhedrin, glad to have had the honor of suffering humiliation for the sake of the name" (Ac. 5:41).

The real issue in our relationship with God is not just the experience of fear. Fear, like anger, is an inevitable and natural human response in the face of danger. Jesus shared our fear of suffering and death in his agony in the garden: "In his anguish he prayed even more earnestly, and his sweat fell to the ground like great drops of blood" (Lk. 22:44). Although Jesus experienced our fear, he did not allow himself to be ruled by it: "Father, if you are willing, take this cup away from me. Nevertheless, let your will be done, not mine" (Lk. 22:43). As Jim Forrest notes, we must realize that violence, long before it touches the body, first destroys the spiritual life of its victims through fear. As with anger, we must not suppress or try to deny our fear; we must strive to bring our fears into conscious prayer before God. We must strive to get to know them in a new way, to glimpse a way to free ourselves from their grasp on our lives.

I have found two prayers to be helpful in my struggle to free myself from the grip of fear. The first is an Advent collect that reads: "Remove the blindness that can not know you. Relieve the fear that hides me from your sight." Fear can blind us to the true nature of God and keep us from entering into the presence of God in prayer. This Advent prayer recognizes that to be freed from our fears is a special grace that God can give us. But Jesus has made it very clear that we will not receive this grace unless we ask for it.

The second prayer that has helped me is the declaration that Paul makes in Romans: "The spirit you received is not the spirit of slaves bringing fear into your lives again; it is the spirit of sons [and daughters], and it makes us cry out, 'Abba!'" (Rm. 8:15). *Abba* is a word like daddy, or mommy. That is how distant our God of love is from the god of fear.

From my own experience as a prisoner of war in Germany during World War II, I concluded that fear is the primary weapon that evil people use to paralyze the good and prevent their liberation. As long as we remain in the grip of fear, we are prisoners of the night: we stand not with the shepherds but with Herod's soldiers. When I was a seventeen-year-old volunteer, I remember attending an indoctrination session for infantry soldiers in which we were told that in order to be good soldiers we had to hate the enemy. In my naive and youthful enthusiasm, I protested, saying that as a Christian I should love my enemy. I could serve in the war because I saw it as just, but I had to pray for the soul of anyone I killed in combat. I ended up going into combat overseas as a private, not even a private first-class. Following my release from the prisoner-of-war camp, I was promoted to the rank of private first-class by an act of Congress. I am grateful to God to this day that I received the courage to speak up.

A critical moment in my understanding of the role of faith in helping us to achieve freedom from fear occurred while I was in the prison camp. The camp was ruled by fear. Because of their fear of us, our Nazi guards deliberately starved us to keep us weak and controllable. Each day we were given only some thin soup and one small potato, and sometimes, especially when we were being transported in freight cars, we had nothing to eat or drink for days at a time. At one point I weighed only eighty pounds.

One day an SS officer took a group of us prisoners to a farm where he was raising mink. As we chopped wood, a slave laborer from eastern Europe was mixing a mash for the animals that had carrots and potatoes in it. He saw how emaciated we were, and while the guard's back was turned he reached into the mash and threw me a potato. That prisoner risked his life to feed me, a stranger. Another time I had seen an SS guard shoot someone down for a similar act, so I tried to signal my gratitude secretly. He smiled at me, and with great deliberation made the sign of the cross. That sign of the cross was like a streak of lightning that lit up the night! It was that man's faith in Jesus that gave him the courage to risk death in order to feed a stranger. I date my vocation to the priesthood from that moment. I envied the man's faith and that freedom from the control of fear. From that day to this, my chief prayer has been: Lord grant me the grace to know your will and the courage to do it! Free me from the spirit of fear!

What can we gay and lesbian people do to free ourselves from the grip of fear on our lives? First, we can form intimate, loving communities; communities of friends who can share moments of sorrow and pain, anger and frustration, as well as moments of joy and play.

I am reminded of Pete Seeger's song "Old Devil Time," a song deeply loved by gay people because it speaks so deeply to our experience:

Old Devil Time, I'm goin' to fool you now!
Old Devil Time, you'd like to bring me down!
When I'm feeling low, my lovers gather 'round
And help me rise to fight you one more time!

Old Devil Fear, you with your icy hands,
Old Devil Fear, you'd like to freeze me cold!
But when I'm afraid my lovers gather 'round
And help me rise to fight you one more time!

Old Devil Pain, you often pinned me down,
You thought I'd cry, and beg you for the end.
But at that very time my lovers gather 'round
And help me rise to fight you one more time!

Old Devil Hate, I knew you long ago,
Then I found out the poison in your breath.
Now when we hear your lies my lovers gather 'round
And help me rise to fight you one more time!

No storm or fire can ever beat us down,
No wind that blows but carries us further on.
And you who fear, o lovers, gather 'round
And we can rise, and sing it one more time!

("Old Devil Time," by Pete Seeger, © 1969 by Fall River
Music, Inc., and Sigma Productions. All rights reserved.
Used by permission.)

We gay people must never let ourselves be driven back into the closet and isolated from one another. We need to call on each other to "gather 'round."

We also need a profound personal awareness of God's love for us, but that awareness can only be achieved through a daily personal encounter with God in prayer.

I've always loved the symbolism of the baseball diamond: we venture out fearfully to first, second, and third base where we can be "out," but eventually we reach home base where we are "safe." Jesus calls us home to a place that is free from fear: "Make your home in me, as I make mine in you" (Jn. 15:4). It is answering this call that will free us from the dominion of fear and lead us into the home of love. For home is the place where true intimacy can happen, where we can experience the perfect love which John tells us drives out all fears, the divine love in which we are all invited to participate.

As Nouwen observes, the tragedy is that we are so possessed by fear that we cannot see our innermost selves as an intimate place to come home to: "We try to find that intimate place in knowledge, competence, notoriety, success, friends, sensations, pleasures, dreams, or artificially induced states of consciousness. Thus we become strangers to ourselves, people who have an address but are never home and hence can never be addressed by the true voice of love."[9] Just as children can let go of their nightmares when they are held in the loving arms of their parents, so we too can let go of all our fears if we can place ourselves in the arms of a God who loves us. The practice of daily prayer will help us to seek our home where Jesus is waiting for us, in our own hearts.

Almighty God, our Mother and our Father, freedom from fear is one of the most precious gifts you offer us. Help us gay men and lesbian women to overcome all the fears that prevent us from being able to accept ourselves, come out of the closet, and be courageously available to one another in this time of crisis. Teach us to fearlessly celebrate our existence and to reach out to share that celebration with all our brothers and sisters! Amen.

7

Lifting the Burden of Guilt, Shame, and Self-Hate

What proves that God loves us is that Christ died for us while we were still sinners.

Romans 5:8

In my twenty years as a pastoral counselor and psychotherapist to lesbians and gays, I have found that the chief threat to the psychological and spiritual health of most gay people, especially those who come from a strong Christian background, is guilt with its companions shame and low self-esteem, which can in turn develop into self-hate. The danger of destructive guilt and shame has always accompanied every step of gay and lesbian human development. With the AIDS crisis, many gays have also regressed to the old patterns of guilt and shame that the gay liberation movement has worked to dissipate. With every new homophobic statement made by television evangelists, the Roman Catholic church hierarchy, and other church spokespersons, many gay and lesbian Christians experience a sharp set-back in their effort to achieve self-acceptance and mental health. In a newspaper interview quoted in the *National Catholic Reporter* (4

April 1988), Cardinal John O'Connor of New York is quoted as saying that he did not encourage the AIDS patients he visited at St. Claire's Hospital "to deny their guilt" as a way of easing their mental pain. Rather, he said, he spent the time "helping them feel guilty for having destroyed their lives and in some cases having destroyed the lives of their families and then helping them find how to handle their guilt." It is thus not surprising that many gay men with AIDS, and many others beset by the fear of AIDS, have returned to a kind of religion they abandoned with good reason in childhood, one that worships a wrathful and vindictive God and that necessarily entails a negative self-image. Unconsciously, they hope that their self-punishment can stave off the onset of the disease or even death itself.

With the AIDS crisis, a new variety of guilt and shame have emerged for gay people: the guilt and shame of being a survivor. Those who have not been stricken with the disease ask themselves, Why are men with purer, more loving hearts than mine suffering with AIDS while I am not? Survivor's guilt is based on the unconscious fear that one's survival has been made possible by the other's illness or death. As a result, any enjoyment of life seems suspect, as if one's happiness had been bought at the price of another's suffering.

To live with an unconscious burden of guilt, shame, and self-hate is to live under continual stress. As I noted earlier, this continual stress can take years off one's life. Unrelieved emotional stress can produce high blood pressure, ulcers, strokes, heart attacks, colitis, asthma, allergic responses, and immune deficiency. Some experts have indicated that a second factor other than the HIV virus may be necessary to explain why some people with the virus come down with AIDS and others do not. I have wondered if that second factor might have something to do with the presence of continual stress due in part to unconscious guilt, which over a lifetime can impair one's immune system and therefore one's health. Stress of this sort can result from taking the homophobic statements of one's church too seriously. In the interests of health, one should struggle to free oneself from the influence of such homophobic authority. Everyone has a serious moral obligation to do whatever is necessary to protect their mental and physical health.

To deal adequately with the issues of guilt and shame, I must make a detour into psychological theory concerning their origin in order to put the specific issues faced by lesbian and gay people in context.

The Origins of Guilt and Shame

The American Heritage Dictionary of the English Language lists two basic definitions of the word *guilt*. The first is "the fact of being responsible for an offense or wrong-doing." Guilt of this kind deals with objective facts that can be ascertained and verified. The second definition is much more subjective and refers not to a fact but a feeling: "remorseless awareness of having done something wrong." This is the kind of guilt with which we are dealing here, a psychic phenomenon, a question of subjective feelings. Notice that the definition itself implies a neurotic quality by defining the feeling as "remorseless." This form of guilt is ruthless, relentless, merciless, and unforgiving.

Shame, in turn, is defined by the dictionary as "a painful situation excited by guilt, disgrace etc." Shame is a "master emotion" that regulates and inhibits the expression of all other feelings. Shameful feelings are aroused most intensely when we see ourselves violating in some way the most basic values with which we identify. It becomes psychologically dangerous when it starts to color our most basic ideas about who we are and how worthy we are. Pathological shame takes the form of self-loathing and self-hatred.

A normal sense of shame can result when, for example, a secret that one feels is embarrassing and humiliating becomes generally known. Shame becomes pathological when that same feeling arises with every rebuke or small failure or begins to color all our relationships because we feel flawed in some essential way. For example, one might be ashamed of one's need for love and affection and see it as weakness.

Freud believed that all civilization was based on guilt; that the price of civilizing a society was paid in forfeiting happiness through a heightened sense of guilt. Freud, at this stage in this thinking, equated happiness with the fulfillment of the irrational and potentially disruptive urge of the id toward pleasure, and he equated civilization with the restraints placed on the id by the superego. This in turn contributed to the conservative mind-set which holds that sexual fulfillment will lead to barbarism and that moral rectitude is based on human sexual frustration. This outlook is in direct contradiction to the premise I have stated throughout this book: that the glory of God is human beings fully alive, and this means sexually alive as well. The true basis of civilization is a healthy psyche whose energies are not thwarted by self-repression and self-hatred but are rather free to celebrate life.

Freud's great positive contribution to our understanding of psychology was to make us aware of the unconscious role that guilt and shame play in our lives. For whenever guilt and shame are unconscious, they work themselves out in self-destructive ways. Unconscious guilt creates a need to make amends, to set things right by masochistically punishing the self in order to remove the vague threat of punishment from without.

It is important to remember, however, that guilt and shame, like anger and fear, are normal, everyday human experiences. Our first task must be to learn how to distinguish between pathological and healthy guilt and shame. Healthy guilt and shame can provide powerful and necessary motivation for human growth and development. They are a special form of anxiety that reminds us of our essential relationship with others. The total absence of any feelings of guilt or shame indicates a psychopathic condition that is the most dehumanizing form of mental illness. We should accept and identify with our healthy feelings of guilt and shame and use them as motives for positive choices and actions.

On the other hand, we must bring into full consciousness all pathological feelings of guilt and shame and attempt to fight off their ability to control our feelings and our actions. Pathological guilt and shame are always destructive of our ability to grow and develop into our full humanness both psychologically and spiritually.

In distinguishing pathological guilt from healthy guilt, we can note that healthy guilt has the following characteristics: it is conscious; the offence that produced it—an action in conflict with our own conscious values—is clear; we know what we must do to remedy the offence; and once we do it, we can let go of the feelings of guilt and shame, we can forgive ourselves.

The source of pathological guilt feelings is usually unconscious. The offence for which we feel guilty is not clear. We feel bad but we don't know exactly why. Pathological guilt leads us to act out in self-destructive ways. We punish ourselves in order to escape the judgment and punishment we unconsciously fear will come from outside ourselves. But no matter what we do, we can't seem to rid ourselves of the feelings of guilt and shame. Even when the person we feel we have offended forgives us, we can't forgive ourselves.

Because of this kind of guilt, some gay men can enjoy sex only in a public place such as a subway toilet, where their sexual activity gives rise to intense guilt and shame and where there is always the possibility of their being mugged or arrested—in other words, a real possibility of being punished. If they have an opportunity for sex in a safe, private place, then they cannot become aroused. Their unconscious fear is that if the possibiltiy of human punishment is not a part of their guilt-laden sexual activity, then God will punish them in some more terrible way.

I recall one client who was terribly guilty on an unconscious level about the murderous anger she felt toward her mother. One Christmas when she planned to visit her mother, she set out for the airport three different times and her ambivalence led her to miss her flight each time. On another occasion I set out to give a talk which I was not sure would be in accord with my orders from Rome. The day before I was scheduled to speak, I took some books out of my car to begin preparing for the talk, slipped, fell, and broke my ankle. That broken ankle resolved my ambivalence. Issues that we cannot resolve on a conscious level because of guilt get resolved unconsciously, most often in a way that is self-destructive.

Psychologists of the object-relations school see the earliest origins of unconscious guilt in the striving of the infant to win parental approval. The infant instinctively takes in and identifies with the will of the mother. For example, the child sees a bright shiny knife and reaches for it. Mother slaps his hand and he pulls back. Later, the child's mother is out of the room. Once again the child is attracted by the bright shiny knife. But now an inner voice says no, and the child restrains his impulse to pick up the knife. Slowly but surely, through thousands of such interactions between child and parent, the child internalizes the values and the will of the parent. This exchange between parent and child is not always on the conscious level. In fact, the child is extremely sensitive to the parent's unconscious superego. For example, if the parent is ashamed of his or her body, the child will pick this up and become ashamed of his or her own body in turn. Parents burdened with guilt-laden superegos quite unwittingly tend to pass on this burden of guilt to their children. Whole areas of natural human feeling such as assertiveness, anger, and sexual feelings can be burdened with pathological guilt. If you listen closely enough to the voice of your superego when it emerges into consciousness, you will hear it speak to you in the voice of your parent. My superego has an Irish brogue.

This earliest form of guilt and shame is tied in with the child's need for and absolute dependence on the affection, acceptance, and love of his or her parents. This kind of unconscious guilt can contain many healthy elements. For example, it is not safe to grasp a sharp knife or to cross the street without looking both ways. I would compare our inheritance of unconscious guilt from our parents to finding an old chest in the attic. One should throw out the old newspapers, hanks of hair, and children's shoes, but if there is a gold brick, hold on to it! We should attempt to bring all our feelings of guilt and shame into consciousness and then let our conscious ego, with a clear sense of its values, sort through these feelings and decide which are worth holding on to and which should be challenged and overcome because they are destructive of the quality of our life.

One primitive source of pathological guilt that occurs in childhood is what I referred to earlier as the "Keeping-Mother-Good" syndrome. W. Ronald Fairbairn in his book *Psychoanalytic Studies of the Personality* makes the famous observation that every child knows at heart that "it is better to be a sinner in a world ruled by a good God than to be a saint in a world ruled by the Devil."[1] Fairbairn points out that to be a sinner in a world ruled by God may be bad, but there is always some sense of security to be derived from the fact that the surrounding world is good; in any case there is always hope of redemption. In a world ruled by the devil, however, the individual may escape being a sinner, but he or she will feel bad anyhow because the world around is bad. Furthermore, there is no sense of security and no hope of redemption—the only prospect is one of death and destruction.

Just as the faithful will do everything in their power to keep their image of God good and take responsibility for all evil onto themselves, so a child will do everything to keep mother good and transfer all the badness onto him- or herself. If the child's mother is evil and abuses the child, the child will think: I must be terrible to make mother act like this! This tactic has the advantage of giving the child a sense of control: if I stop being so bad, mother will stop abusing me. Also, if the child truly saw his or her mother as evil, the only choice would be to withdraw from reality altogether through a psychotic breakdown. Keeping mother good is the only way the child has of staying in touch with reality.

While the Keeping-Mother-Good syndrome may be a healthy adaptation for a child with abusive parents, in later life it has a tendency to become a disastrous kind of masochism. Often it remains the primary way in which that person responds to all abuse for the rest of his or her adult life. Once the gay or lesbian person with this syndrome reaches the stage of development where they become aware of their sexual orientation, they frequently tie their guilt, shame, and low self-esteem to their gayness. We can recognize this kind of defense in the gay or lesbian person who hangs on to a destructive relationship with an alcoholic or abusive partner, or who remains in a job where he or she is treated abusively and unjustly. People with this problem see their abusive partner or lousy job as the only possible choice and feel they must make the best of it, and therefore turn all their anger in on themselves. We may have to make the best of the parents we get in childhood, but we can always change jobs and even partners, if necessary.

This defense was exhibited by a client of mine whose bicycle was stolen by a neighborhood bully. When my client realized who had taken his bicycle, he felt powerless to get it back and fell into a murderous rage. Feeling guilty about his anger, and taking the precept of "turning the other cheek" somewhat too far, he invited the thief into his apartment and gave him his television set. The only way he could deal with his rage was by turning it in on himself, making himself the wrongdoer and punishing himself for his anger. A religious precept of forgiveness masked a masochistic self-hatred.

This incident has an amusing ending. Returning to his old neighborhood after having been away for several years, my client ran into the same neighborhood bully. The man grabbed hold of him and asked, "Are you the one who gave me the television?" When my client said yes, the bully took out his wallet and gave him fifty dollars, saying: "Here, take this! I'm no sleaze-bag! I have principles too!"

The Capacity for Concern

There is still another kind of guilt that tends to be healthy and conscious rather than destructive. D. W. Winnicott explained this form of guilt in his essay "The Development of the Capacity for Concern."[2] What we refer to negatively as guilt also has a positive aspect, which Winnicott calls concern or "ruth." Concern refers to the fact that the individual *cares* or *minds* about others, feels a sense of responsibility, and accepts the consequences of his or her actions. A capacity for concern is at the basis of all constructive play and work and is, contrary to Freud's understanding, the real basis of civilization.

In order for a child to develop a sense of concern, he or she must have adequate parenting. From earliest infancy every child is what Winnicott calls a "symbiotic therapist." (A symbiotic therapist is one who tries to heal another by absorbing the other person's pain.) When an infant uses his or her mother solely to relieve hunger, the mother becomes for the child what Winnicott calls the "object mother." That aspect of the mother that meets the child's demands for nourishment and goes on to provide care and affection Winnicott refers to as the "environmental mother." The urge to relieve hunger leads the child to a ruthless exploitation of the mother as object, but having done so, the child feels a sense of guilt which is later allayed by the contribution the child can make to the environmental mother. For example, if the mother is feeling depressed, the child will smile at the mother in an effort to lift her depression. If for some reason the mother is not physically and emotionally present for the child, then the child is deprived of the opportunity to make reparation for his or her demands and will become ashamed of his/her body and its impulses.

Adult sexual partners also deal with each other both as sexual objects who mutually attack and consume each other and as environmental objects who survive this attack and remain loving, affectionate, and eager to make reparation for any damage done. I have always admired the wisdom of my professor of moral theology who, when asked what kind of foreplay was morally acceptable between sexual partners, responded: "Whatever is mutually agreeable and agreeably mutual."

Moral Education and Guilt

The central therapeutic issue in moral development is how to undertake moral education without producing an unwanted by-product of massive guilt and shame. There are ways of morally educating a child that are fundamentally destructive to human growth because they eliminate autonomy—the possibility of personal choice—and thus eliminate personal responsibility. The child who receives such an upbringing is not an autonomous, responsible, moral individual, but an obedient, irresponsible conformist.

We have a desperate moral need, especially in the lesbian and gay community, for individuals who are able and willing to be models of how to make a personal decision about their way of life without undue guilt and shame and take adult responsibility for that decision. One of my clients told me that he used to experience intense shame every time he gave money to a street beggar. He was finally able to break free from that shame when he located its childhood origin: his father had once called him a fool when he generously gave a toy to a playmate.

There is a basic trend in every person toward autonomy, toward being spontaneous and self-governing. However, many factors exert a pressure on us to let our lives be determined by outside expectations rather than inner conviction. For gay people, those outside expectations try to get us to hide or repress our difference and conform to heterosexist roles and behavior. Thank God we all have fallible parents! Through their mistakes, they force us to take stock of our lives, grow up, make personal decisions, and take responsibility for them. Thank God, too, for the fallibility of the human church—otherwise we could never distance ourselves from it and mature spiritually.

The person who has been subjected in childhood to excessive demands and expectations does not become self-governing, but can only react to what is expected. One can either conform or rebel; both of these choices are reactions to the external rather than the internal, and both result in an increase of shame and guilt.

The fiercest morality is that of early infancy. For the infant, immorality takes the form of compliance at the expense of the infant's personal well-being. Compliance brings immediate rewards, and adults mistake compliance for growth only too easily. The process of maturation can be bypassed by a series of identifications so that one develops a false self, a copy of someone else, perhaps, and what can be called the true or essential self becomes hidden and deprived of living experience. Winnicott observes that "the child knows in his bones that it is *hope* that is locked up in wicked behavior, and that *despair* is linked with compliance and false socialization."[3] If children sense that they can act out their true self, even when that self is angry or wants something contrary to the wish of their parents, and can still be loved, then they can believe that their true self is lovable.

The Family Referee

In his book *Psychotherapy and Growth: A Family Systems Perspective*,[4] W. Robert Beavers deals with the destructive use of shame and guilt within the family. What Beavers describes as the mid-range family (that is, the average family, with some serious neurotic problems, that is somewhere between the optimal family in which there is excellent mental health and the dysfunctional family) frequently behaves as if an invisible referee, a shared external authority, were present. The referee may be abstract or personified. In many families it is a "they," that faceless order of good people who have controlled themselves properly and, therefore, possess social power. In others, it is a formal religious code adhered to with perfectionistic inhumanity. The referee tyrannizes all members of the family through standards of thought, behavior, and feelings that are pathetically insensitive to people's needs, especially sexual and aggressive needs.

The referee system does not stop at behavioral control, but disciplines feeling and thought as well, continually trying to bring everyone's inner life into agreement with the rules. Much of the self must thus be expressed in forbidden fantasy or illicit behavior (such as masturbation) which lead to intense shame and guilt. The family referee differs from the superego because the "shoulds" and "oughts" are shared by all family members. There is no I, only a "we."

The referee reduces the autonomy of all members. All individual thinking, feeling, and action are suspect. If any member is different in any way from the rest of the family, this produces intense anxiety and a concerted effort to deny or repress the difference. People who differ from the family's expectations are caught between resentment if they conform and guilt if they rebel; there is little room for any satisfaction or pleasure in life. The gay or lesbian child in a midrange family will be forced to conform to family patterns under threat of emotional rejection and even physical punishment.

Frequently we project the family referee onto God, so that God becomes a transcendent superego before whom we are totally exposed and, consequently, in whose presence we feel guilt and shame. It was this understanding of God that led Sartre, the French existentialist philosopher, to identify belief in God with the most extreme form of guilt and shame. The very concept, Sartre argues, that we are always present to the eye of God, whose vision penetrates to our inmost being, is a source of intolerable shame: "The other [i.e., God] looking at me is hell!"[5] This statement would be true if that look were an objectifying look of judgment by a God of fear, measuring us against some impossible moral standard. There can be no healthy intimacy where we feel that we are exposing our self to intense shame and guilt. But Sartre overlooks the possibility that a father's or mother's look—or God's look, for that matter—can be one of unconditional love.

In midrange families, the definition of what is good or acceptable often excludes much that is human. To be angry is bad; to have sexual feelings of any kind, gay or straight, is often unacceptable; and even to have ambivalent feelings about one's parents—in other words, to see them as both good and bad and therefore to have feelings of both love and anger for them—is strongly disapproved. This last feature is extremely damaging to the possibility of pleasant family interactions and peace of mind. Rather than accept that ambivalence is natural and at the heart of being human, midrange families perceive it as part of a willful and evil self that must be brought under control.

One of my clients once told me of his most intense childhood experience of shame. At a family reunion when he was ten, he decided to put on a surprise entertainment for the entire family. He made up a tutu from his mother's clothing, put the music of his favorite ballet on the record player, and danced into the living room in front of all the guests. What for him was a joyful expression of the feminine side of his nature was obviously a painful embarrassment to his parents and relatives. To this day he is afraid of all spontaneity, fearful that any such gesture will reveal his femininity and induce feelings of fierce guilt, shame, and self-hate.

Entire families can share feelings of shame over events such as a suicide or bankruptcy, or because of an alcoholic parent or a lesbian daughter or gay son. The family's implicit rule becomes not to talk about painful experiences of any kind. A sense of shame leads them to rigidly control their emotions and to set demanding, inhuman standards for themselves. As a result they never expose or share deep feelings.

We all experience longings and rebellious feelings because we have suppressed aspects of ourselves that do not fit in with our family or society. The midrange family's referee places an additional burden on a developing child, especially if that child is lesbian or gay, which results in a narrow self-definition and larger repressed areas.

This narrow self-definition is frequently expressed in the stereotypical male and female social roles accepted by the family as morally correct and divinely sanctioned. The gay or lesbian child brought up in such a family will be made to feel intense shame and guilt if he or she shows any desire to deviate from those stereotypical roles. The effeminate boy or the tom-boy girl will be forced to suppress their true self and play out a false, conforming self in order to be accepted in their family. How often, for example, a boy who would like to develop a musical talent is forced to join the Little League, and how often the girl who would love to play in the Little League is forced to stay at home and play house.

The midrange family will frequently ridicule and make fun of the male child's need for support and comfort, calling him a "mama's boy" or "sissy." When such a child becomes an adult, to feel a need for support, attention, physical contact, or to feel in any way weak, dependent, or needy becomes a source of intense shame.

One client sent to me by his parish priest was a man in his fifties who, although biologically male, felt psychologically like a female. For fifty years he had attempted to repress and deny what he felt was his real female self. He married, raised a family, and held down a job. He was an excellent father to his children because, as he put it, they had two mothers without knowing it. Finally, at the age of fifty, he could no longer continue to repress his female self. He felt his only choice was to become the female he always was or commit suicide. He informed his wife and children of his decision and began to dress and act as a female. To his surprise, he found that, instead of rejecting him as he anticipated, his family was able to share the joy of his liberation. Moreover, many of his fellow workers, delighted by his courage, were able because of his example to explore repressed areas in their own lives. (The irony of this situation is that my client and his/her wife became a lesbian couple sacramentally united in marriage.)

The Role of Therapy

In the past, the primary therapeutic method used to try to change homosexuals into heterosexuals was to intensify their guilt, shame, and self-hatred. In their attempts to "convert" their homosexual clients, homophobic therapists have used the same techniques on a conscious level that midrange families use unconsciously. This effort at conversion is based on a number of false assumptions. The first is that all human beings are by nature heterosexual. Consequently, homosexuality is explained as a failure in psychosexual development and is equated with "immaturity." Maturity, in turn, is defined as genital attraction to the opposite sex. From this perspective, a heterosexual rapist is seen as essentially more mature than a homosexual or lesbian expressing genuine human love in a sexual relationship.

The second assumption is that sexual orientation is a matter of choice and that one could, if properly motivated, choose to change it. The way to bring about that change, according to Edmund Bergler in his classical work *Homosexuality: Disease or Way of Life?*, is to "mobilize any latent feelings of guilt."[6] And if no change in sexual orientation occurs, the therapist can blame it on the client's failure of will, which then causes the client more guilt, shame, and self-hatred.

In an identical fashion, those religious groups that claim to be able to "heal" homosexuals attempt to do so by intensifying the gay or lesbian person's sense of being sinful and evil because of their sexual feelings. Since sexual orientation is fundamentally unchangeable, the best that can be hoped for from this process is that the gay person will suppress his or her gay identity and adopt behavior that is in conflict with that identity, which is in effect a form of psychic mutilation or suicide. The implicit judgment is that it is better to be a sick heterosexual than a healthy homosexual.

The assumptions underlying this form of treatment are false. Homosexuality is a natural variant of human sexuality. Homosexuals are capable of achieving completely mature, loving, healthy relationships. The empirical evidence upholds the position that it is impossible to change one's sexual orientation. One can repress or deny it; one can choose to act in a way that contradicts it; but the orientation itself cannot be changed. Since there is no evidence of a successful change in orientation, the attempt to do so results in the creation of pseudo-heterosexuals. The majority of those who undergo treatment of this sort end up seriously damaged by the treatment because of increased gender dysphoria. The American Psychological Association now recognizes the fact that mental illness can result from being in conflict with one's sexual orientation. Thus the only route to mental health is to learn to accept and live in a positive way with one's orientation.

Coming Out

The process of lifting the burden of guilt, shame, and low self-esteem for a lesbian or gay person is identical to the process of "coming out." In his article "Developmental Stages of the Coming Out Process,"[7] Eli Coleman identifies five stages in the development of a positive gay identity. The first stage is a pre-coming-out stage. If gay identity is fully established by the age of three, as most experts believe, family members will be aware of the child's sexual orientation even at that early age. Most children learn from their families that homosexuality is wrong and that they are expected to marry when they grow up. Consequently, the child feels different—alienated and alone. Acknowledging same-sex feelings would result in ridicule and rejection; thus gay and lesbian children develop low self-esteem and protect themselves through defences such as denial and repression. The consequences of this concealment can be enormously destructive. Every time gay or lesbian children repress their true feelings they injure themselves psychically. As a result they suffer from depression and experience less vitality and joy in life.[8]

Because children are not consciously aware of same-sex feelings, they can only communicate their inner conflict between their feelings and the expectation of their family through behavioral problems such as psychosomatic illnesses and suicide attempts. The only way through to a healthy resolution of these problems is to courageously face the fact of being different, break down one's defences, and acknowledge one's lesbian or gay orientation.

Most gays and lesbians become consciously aware of their sexual orientation during puberty, that is, between the ages of thirteen and eighteen. Once one has become aware of same-sex feelings, a period of time usually elapses before one is able to label them as such. As a result, adolescents may be confused when they try to identify their feelings, but this does not imply that their sexual orientation has not already been determined.

The process of coming out—telling others that one is lesbian or gay—is identical with the process of self-acceptance. The risk involved is weighed against the need for external validation. If the person chosen as confidant reacts negatively, then all our feelings of shame and guilt will be reconfirmed. If, however, we receive a positive reception, then we can begin the healing process of accepting our sexual feelings and building our self-esteem.

Empirical evidence has established that a positive lesbian or homosexual identity is necessary for healthy psychological adjustment.[9] One of the primary functions of gay social and religious groups is to provide the "accepting environment" in which one can learn to accept and love oneself as gay. Acceptance, originally denied us in the family setting, is not something that we can give ourselves; rather, it is something we give each other.

One of my clients, a young man who had made several suicide attempts, tried three times to attend a Dignity liturgy. Each time he walked back and forth in front of the church, but his fear and anxiety were too great to allow him to enter. Finally, on his fourth attempt he managed to walk in. That act of courage broke through his defensive fears and he quickly began to rebuild his self-esteem and self-acceptance in therapy.

One must take risks to gain acceptance from others and, thus, to be able to accept oneself. In fact, it is the realization that coming out will be a source of intense pain to their families that prevents many gays and lesbians from beginning the process. They would rather absorb all the pain themselves and keep their same-sex feelings a dark secret. It was this fear of hurting his parents that lay behind the suicide attempts of the young man I mentioned above. Parents should realize that when gay sons or lesbian daughters come out, they are facing a terrible risk of rejection. Coming out is always an act of courage and trust.

Because of their vulnerability, it is extremely important that young people be careful in choosing those persons to whom they will risk coming out. They should be reasonably sure in advance that that person will be accepting. Frequently, the best person with whom to begin that process is a carefully selected therapist.

Effective psychotherapy for gay people must challenge all family referee systems, question the underlying premise of human depravity, and offer an experience of intimacy without preconditions. The therapist's task is to help gay clients recognize and accept their gay identity, improve their interpersonal and social functioning, and value and integrate their gay identity while living in a frequently hostile heterosexual society.

For a lesbian or gay person, a natural part of the healing process in therapy may involve having intense feelings of guilt and shame rise into consciousness. Most of my work as a psychotherapist with gay clients centers around creating the therapeutic environment and the trust which will allow them to risk bringing all their guilt and shame and self-hatred into consciousness and to share these feelings in a loving, nonjudgmental atmosphere. By means of this process they frequently succeed in exorcising the demons of pathological guilt and self-hate and begin to achieve the energy, peace, and joy of self-acceptance.

The most effective antidote to shame is the ability to laugh at oneself. Those of my clients who were able to laugh at their own accounts of feeling humiliated experienced an immediate alleviation of their feelings of shame. Humor has always been one of the healthiest features of the gay community.

Once a gay or lesbian person has become part of a community of accepting friends with whom he or she can share their joys and sorrows as gay people, it is much easier to withstand the rejection of other friends, family members, and society without intense shame and guilt. Since the chances that one will meet with immediate positive acceptance on the part of parents and other family members are slim, it is usually best to have a solid basis in an accepting community before coming out.

Most families need to go through a period of mourning before they can accept a homosexual son or daughter. They must pass through the stages of denial, compromise, depression, self-blaming, anger, and so on before they can arrive at the positive acceptance of their gay son or lesbian daughter. Parents must grieve the loss of the image of their son or daughter as married and having children. It is important for gay people to persevere with their parents and family members as they go through that grieving process, realizing how long they themselves took to achieve self-acceptance. It is a great help for a family going through this process to be able to share their feelings of anger, guilt, pain, and fear with other parents of gay children through organizations such as PFLAG, Parents and Friends of Lesbians and Gays. The majority of clients I have worked with during the coming-out process have, after a period of mourning, been accepted positively by their families.

Parents of gay sons or lesbian daughters are not responsible for their children's sexual orientations. But parents *can* be responsible in part for whether or not their gay son or lesbian daughter is a psychologically healthy, self-accepting person or continues in a life of guilt, shame, and self-hatred.

The next stage of the coming-out process involves experimentation with one's newly established sexual identity, a period that is akin to adolescence. This period often comes late for gay people. I have had clients who did not seek out their first sexual relationship until their thirties or forties. The opportunity to interact with peers who are open and honest about their sexual orientation helps one to develop a positive self-image. Thus the primary developmental task at this stage is to learn how to meet and socialize with other gay and lesbian people and to develop a positive sense of one's own sexual attractiveness to others. Frequently one must resolve serious problems with one's body image. For example, one might think, I am too fat/too thin to be attractive to anyone; or, I am too feminine/too butch. Organizations such as the Girth and Mirth Society have come into being to help people support each other while they deal with their body image. Gay people frequently have an intense fear of intimacy because they think that the real self that they have carefully hidden and are ashamed of will not be lovable.

Adolescents with low self-esteem have a greater tendency to act in self-destructive ways. They run the risk of refusing to take responsibility for their lives, preferring to feel sorry for themselves and blame others. They must learn that the worst obstacle to successful self-acceptance lies in themselves.

A great danger at this stage is to become dependent on alcohol or drugs to relieve chronic psychological pain and shore up a weak self-image. Three out of ten gay men have serious problems with alcohol. Compulsive sexual activity, which frequently takes place while one is drunk or high, can also be used to bolster one's self-image. But this activity is usually followed by even more intense guilt, shame, and self-hatred, and the resulting increase in negative feelings leads to a more compulsive need to escape once again through drink, drugs, and compulsive sexual activity. Today, that compulsive sexual activity carries with it the added menace of exposure to the AIDS virus.[10]

A word of caution is in order here. Although the only way to healthy self-acceptance is through a process of coming out, not all acts of coming out are necessarily well motivated. One can come out to parents, for example, with the intention of hurting them in order to obtain a kind of revenge. This kind of coming out only leads to greater guilt and lower self-esteem. Or one can come out imprudently at work where one's unconscious motive is to punish oneself masochistically by getting fired. We must carefully analyze motives for coming out in any particular situation to be sure they will lead to a healthier sense of self-acceptance.

Usually after a period of sexual and social experimentation, a gay man or lesbian woman will yearn for a more stable, committed relationship that combines both physical and emotional attraction. As Coleman points out, first relationships are frequently disastrous for many reasons. One cannot build a healthy, lasting relationship if one still harbors feelings of self-hatred and shame. To have a successful relationship, one must have made a good start toward a consolidated, positive self-identity. Studies suggest that developing an integrated, positive identity takes the average gay person ten to fourteen years after the first awareness of same-sex feelings.

Being in a relationship makes it difficult to conceal one's lesbian or gay identity from friends, family, and society. Either one must complete the task of coming out or the pressures that result from being in a relationship will become unbearable. I have seen many gay relationships break up because every holiday such as Christmas or Thanksgiving the couple would separate to spend the holiday with their respective families. In another version of this scenario, every time the family visits, the other partner has to move out of the couple's home and remove all traces of his or her presence. This kind of denial and secretiveness, which springs from shame and guilt, can quickly undermine a relationship.

In one's first experience of affectionate intimacy, one tends to become a "hungry infant" who wants to be mothered and demands total attention and gratification. Since no adult can make that kind of commitment, the result will be intense jealousy, possessiveness, and lack of trust. All efforts to assert independence and a need for separateness will be interpreted as a lack of love. Anger will build between the couple until the pain of being together outweighs the pleasure. When this occurs, it usually means that one of the partners, or even both, has not reached the earlier stages of self-acceptance. Guilt, shame, and self-hatred make trust impossible, and one unconsciously projects the self-hatred onto one's partner. Many gay people must go through several tries at a relationship before they can conquer the "hungry infant" and begin to build a more mature relationship. These adult relationships are characterized by nonpossessiveness, mutual trust, and freedom. When a mature relationship ends, it is handled with normal grief reactions and does not become psychologically destructive. Someone with an integrated gay identity has a much better chance of facing all the challenges of midlife and old age without serious psychological problems.

The Religious Dimension

Every step in the coming-out process for lesbian women and gay men involves mourning. One must die to one's old identity and all the possibilities involved with that identity before one can achieve self-acceptance. One must grieve and let go of the hope of belonging to and being accepted by the straight world. Each step in this mourning process, if it is successfully accomplished, opens up the possibility for spiritual growth. As we come to terms with our "exiled" status in this world, we gay men and lesbian women have a wonderful opportunity to develop our faith, trust, and love of God and our sense of belonging fearlessly to the family of God. Many hospital chaplains who minister to people with AIDS have been astonished at the depth of faith and the courage of gay patients facing death. This witness has been so powerful that many of these chaplains have changed their attitude toward homosexuality.

It is possible to feel a healthy form of guilt and shame in the presence of God. In fact, that emotion is identical with the healthy guilt we feel in our dealings with each other. As Jesus said, "in so far as you did this to one of the least of these brothers [and sisters] of mine, you did it to me" (Mt. 25:40). Scripture tells us emphatically that we can be in a true and appropriate relationship to God only if we are conscious of our guilt, repent of it, and seek God's mercy and forgiveness.

As Paul Tournier points out in his excellent work *Guilt and Grace: A Psychological Study,*[11] Scripture reveals a Christ who welcomes those whom the world despises and who are conscious of their guilt; and on the other hand, he speaks severely to those who are self-satisfied and who repress any sense of guilt.

The same criteria for distinguishing healthy from pathological guilt apply equally to our intimate relationship with God. Healthy guilt is conscious; we are aware of the offense; we know what to do to make reparation. Having done so we can accept forgiveness from God, and, consequently, forgive ourselves, restoring our peace of mind and self-esteem.

Healthy guilt in our relation to God is identical in many ways to the healthy guilt an infant feels in relation to his or her parents. Healthy guilt grows out of a personal encounter with a loving God and a need, born out of gratitude, to make reparation and seek forgiveness for any action on our part that separates us from God, our father and mother. Healthy guilt is always in the service of intimacy; it leads to a true and personal relationship with God.

Just as a healthy sense of ruth or concern arises in the interplay between infant and mother, so too a healthy, positive sense of guilt and concern can arise in us when our spiritual life is based on a direct, personal encounter with God. Pathological guilt and shame arise in our spiritual life when we are not aware of God's love and presence, but feel we must earn that love through perfectionistic compliance with an arbitrary and inhuman moral code or law.

There is an equivalent to the coming-out process in our spiritual life, a gradual revealing of our secret self to our parent in heaven. In thus revealing ourselves to God, we take the risk of self-disclosure that is an essential step toward greater intimacy. I agree with Tournier that the "depth of our human misery is that we are never completely certain whether we are obeying or disobeying God."[12] The central prayer of my whole life has been: "Lord give me the grace to know your will, and the courage to do it!" The greatest fear of my life has been that if I did find out what God's will was, I might face an impossible task, such as denying my gayness. My greatest joy and relief, however, has been the discovery that God does not ask the impossible, that God accepts me and loves me exactly as I am.

The most moving spiritual experience I ever had occurred at Mount Savior Monastery. I had been praying for months for guidance from God concerning the Vatican order to give up my ministry to lesbian and gay people. While praying for guidance, I was suddenly inundated with an intense feeling of being loved just as I am, a gay man and a gay priest. That love seemed to heal deep wounds in my psyche, wounds of guilt, shame, and self-loathing, and produced a marvelous, liberating feeling of peace. I had the feeling that God would go with me down whatever road I chose. "Lord, remove the blindness that can not know you; relieve the fear, shame and guilt that hides us from your sight!" I pray for all my readers that they may receive that same grace from God according to their need. Amen.

Part Three

Releasing God's Power

Introduction: Say the Word and I Shall Be Healed

On many occasions in recent years I have had the privilege of presiding at a liturgy of healing for persons with AIDS.[1] As moving as these liturgies have been, they have at the same time challenged my faith and trust in God. They have been the occasion for me to reflect on God's healing role in our lives. In the next three chapters, I want to consider three spiritual virtues that are at the heart of our faith relationship with God, and that have a special significance and a special difficulty for lesbians and gay men. These virtues are *trust, gratitude,* and the *spirit of reconciliation.*

These virtues are of particular interest to us in the time of the AIDS crisis, because in a certain way they are the virtues that give us the means and the power to release God's healing presence in our lives and our world.

8

Trusting in God

Yes, you love all that exists, you hold nothing of what you have made in abhorrence, for had you hated anything, you would not have formed it. And how, had you not willed it, could a thing persist, how be conserved if not called forth by you? You spare all things because all things are yours, Lord, lover of life, you whose imperishable spirit is in all.

Wisdom 11:24–12:1

In the Old Testament we read that a leper, Naaman, came to the prophet Elisha to be healed. Following Elisha's instructions, he plunges seven times in the waters of the Jordan. Finding himself clean of leprosy, he returns to express his gratitude to Elisha, and because he is grateful he receives the gift of faith, saying, "Your servant will no longer offer holocaust or sacrifice to any other god except Yahweh" (2 K. 5:1–19).

As gay people, our faith is above all else involved with the virtue of trust. Hans Küng, in his book *Does God Exist?*, makes the point that the essential human psychological foundation and presupposition for faith is trust. Erik Erikson, the development psychologist, claims that the first task of the human infant is to learn basic trust. This trust is the cornerstone of a psychologically healthy personality; without it a decent human life is impossible. No deep intimacy, no true friendship, no vital faith is possible unless we take the risk of trusting.

A fundamental trust that life is good comes to us as a gift. Infants learn to trust life insofar as they are truly loved and cared for by their parents, but maintaining a sense of fundamental trust is a lifelong task. None of us grows up without some wounding of our ability to trust. Consequently, we must all struggle to achieve the ability to trust. Despite uncertainty, pain, sorrow, sickness, and death, we must trust that life is good and that love can triumph even over the grave. Our last action in life should be an act of loving trust. In the words of the *Te Deum,* "In te Domine speravi, non confundar in aeternum"—In you, Lord, I have hoped. I shall never be let down in all eternity.

The good news of God's self-revelation in Jesus Christ is that no matter how badly wounded our human capacity for trust and love, we can start over; we can be born again through the power of the Holy Spirit. Trustworthiness is the very nature of God. "Even if we are unfaithful, he will still remain faithful, for he cannot deny himself." We are the adopted children of God, and through God's motherly love for us we can restore fundamental trust in our lives.

In the Roman Catholic church, the collect for the liturgy of the twenty-eighth Sunday after Pentecost beautifully expresses our trust as adopted children in our divine parent, God, our mother and our father: "The hand of your loving kindness powerfully yet gently guides all the moments of our day. Go before us in our pilgrimage of life. Anticipate our needs and prevent our falling."

Our challenge as Christians is to allow ourselves, in Matthew Fox's words, "to experience the ecstasy and blessing that all life is; to experience the goodness of all creation and its essential, ultimate trustworthiness." It is this trust that allows us to play all our lives like children in the presence of a loving parent; it allows us to know "the joy and ecstasy of creation, nature, friendship, art, poetry, music, dance, non-compulsive work, non-competitive sport, sexuality in the service of love."

We have God's promise that no matter how much evil exists in our lives, God will see to it that the good that eventually results will far outweigh any evil. This is the meaning of the joyous cry at the Resurrection liturgy on the night of Holy Saturday: O *felix culpa,* O happy sin that resulted in such a marvelous redeemer!

However, I believe that gay men and lesbian women face a unique challenge to their ability to trust creation. Since we do not choose our sexual orientation, we experience it as given, a part of our created reality. Insofar as our experience of our sexual orientation is negative, and we see ourselves as sinful, sick, or evil, we will experience a deep crisis in our ability to trust the Creator. Only a sadistic God, a God who inspires fear, mistrust, and hatred would do such a thing—not a loving God whom one could address as a loving parent.

If we accept the church's fallible teaching in this area, then we have a right to harbor a basic distrust in life. We will develop what I call the "Boys-in-the-Band" syndrome, an attitude of cynicism, self-hate, and mutual cruelty. On top of this, the AIDS crisis threatens to destroy our trust and hope in a God of love and enslave us once again to a god of fear.

A breakdown of our relationship of trust with God inevitably leads to a breakdown of our trust of each other. For some AIDS has become an objective symbol of what they feel to be an intrinsic disorder in our affectionate and loving feelings for each other. All human contact, especially sexual contact, becomes suspect. A paranoid spirit of mutual distrust can enter deeply into our lives, further endangering any possibility of achieving true intimacy with each other. The opposite of trust is despair: despair in life, in love, despair of any true happiness.

Our only alternative is to go the other route, to begin the deepening and hallowing route toward true spiritual growth. We can refuse to believe that the God whose love we experience daily can be sadistic. We can achieve a greater trust of self, body, nature, the cosmos, and God; even a trust that our death, when it comes, is in the natural order of things and will "work unto good," leading us to a new life as Jesus has promised: "Father I want those you have given me to be with me where I am" (Jn. 17:24). As Matthew Fox asks, "Who knows more about the beauty of creation and New Creation than those who have been told verbally and nonverbally by religion and society that the way they were created was a mistake and even sinful!"[1]

This struggle is first of all one to achieve self-trust, a struggle to believe what God is saying to us directly. The primary teacher in the church is the Holy Spirit, and the Spirit dwells in our hearts and speaks to us through our own experience. Second, it is a struggle to see ourselves as persons with divine dignity and responsibility, to see our gayness itself as a blessing and not as a curse, a blessing for which we should be grateful to God. We must learn as gay persons to celebrate our existence. We must learn to take a chance on God.

God, our Father and Mother, our ability to trust life is often deeply wounded. Grant us the grace to experience the basic trustworthiness of our lives as you have created them so we can accept and celebrate our existence as lesbian women and gay men. Help us to trust that you truly love us and accept us as we are. Amen.

9

Thanks Be to God

It seems that no one has come back to give praise to God, except this foreigner.

Luke 17:18

In the Gospel of Luke we read of the time when ten lepers came to Jesus and, keeping the legal distance, cried out to him, "Jesus! Master! Take pity on us." Jesus said to them, "Go and show yourselves to the priests." (The priests were the health officials of the time, and it was they who determined who did and did not have leprosy and, therefore, who could and could not participate in the community.) As they went, they were cured of their leprosy. But only one, a Samaritan, felt gratitude and returned to thank and praise Jesus. Jesus was pained at the ingratitude of the other nine and remarked: "It seems that no one has come back to give praise to God, except this foreigner." As a reward, the grateful Samaritan received an even deeper healing, a healing of his soul: "Your faith has saved you" (Lk. 17:11–19).

In my practice as a psychotherapist, I frequently find that pathological religious faith leads many to base their spiritual life on feelings of guilt and shame. Their primary prayer is one of contrition. Every time they enter the presence of God they experience fear of rejection because of their guilt. Instead of feeling gratitude for the love that God has freely given them, they feel they must earn that love through self-punishment.

A much healthier and more theologically sound spiritual life is one based in gratitude for all the blessings God has given us. As Meister Eckhardt wrote: "If the only prayer you ever say to God in your whole life is a heartfelt thank you, that will suffice." We should deliberately cultivate this spirit of gratitude. Our constant daily prayer should be, *Deo gratias,* thanks be to God; thanks for life and health, for our parents and friends, for beauty and nature, and for our gayness with all the blessings and pains that it brings. Yes, we should thank God for times of darkness and trial, pain and suffering, for these times offer the opportunity for growth and spiritual deepening.

Saint Ignatius Loyola constantly repeated in his spiritual exercises that, although all the good things of this world belong to us for our enjoyment, the glory belongs to God. The practical way we can give glory to God is through the simple virtue of gratitude. Gratitude frees the hand of God to pour out every blessing. A spirit of ingratitude, however, ties God's hands. When those who feel no gratitude receive special blessings from God, they may become proud and self-important, in the mistaken belief that they deserve these blessings because they are better than those around them. The salvation of such people may thus become seriously endangered.

One time when I was visiting members of my family in the west of Ireland, a woman bicycled out from a distant village to see a man who had been cured at Our Lady's shrine at Knock. The man was a local farmer who had broken his back in a fall five years before. For four years his sons carried him to Knock seeking a cure, and every year they carried him back. The fifth year, however, he walked home with his sons. My Irish cousin was amused that the woman on the bicycle had traveled all that distance to see the man. "What will that woman see," my cousin asked, "but a man working in the field? His family needed him, so Our Lady cured him. You can't see a miracle!"

I remember reflecting that in such an atmosphere of faith, humility, trust, and gratitude, God was free to perform miracles without disrupting anyone's life or inflating anyone's ego.

If we are truly grateful, if we know that these blessings come to us because of God's goodness and have nothing to do with our worthiness or unworthiness, then there is no limit to what God can accomplish in us. As Jesus reminds us, "I have come that [you] may have life and have it to the full" (Jn. 10:10).

In the process of mourning whereby we come to accept our exiled status as gay people, there is a danger of getting stuck in the stage of being angry and filled with self-pity. We may thus fail to recognize the many special gifts that come with being gay. Once my clients begin to heal the psychic wounds that give rise to that anger, then the tone of our therapy sessions changes. Instead of remembering all the hurtful acts that gave rise to their anger, they begin to remember the loving and tender moments in the past and to experience a sense of gratitude despite the psychological wounds they had received. This in turn led to a spirit of forgiveness. They were able to forgive themselves, forgive those who had wounded them, and forgive God.

Whenever we gay people gather to celebrate the Eucharist, let us remember that the word *Eucharist* means literally "to give thanks," to express gratitude to God for all God's blessings. A playful poem by Hilaire Belloc expresses the Christian spirit of gratitude:

Wherever a Christian sun doth shine,
There floweth merriment and good red wine.
At least I've always found it so.
Benedicamus Domino.

Thank you, God; thank you for life, even with all its pain, sorrow, and tragedy. Thank you for my gayness, even with all its alienation and suffering, and yet with all its potential for spiritual growth, richness, and blessings. And thank you, God, for all the spiritual families that have enabled us to love ourselves by learning to love each other.

10

Reconciliation and God's Presence

I came into your presence as into the presence of God, but you have received me kindly.

Genesis 33:10

I recently had the privilege of reading Father Edward Schillebeeckx's theological work: *Christ, The Experience of Jesus as Lord.*[1] Father Schillebeeckx's basic thesis is that, in every age, each person must have his or her own experience of Jesus as the Lord, and work out the consequences of that experience within the circumstances of the times in which he or she lives. Many different historical situations have conditioned the various forms that this experience has taken in the past. This is true even in the New Testament itself, where we find many different theologies based on the historical reality of Jesus, each theology a specific response to the needs of the community in which it was formulated. All, however, had as a common theme the active struggle for human liberation.

In keeping with Schillebeeckx's theme, I hope to formulate a theology that is a specific response to the needs of the gay and lesbian community as that community is involved in a struggle for gay human liberation.

In part 4 of his work, entitled "God's Glory and Humanity's Truth, Well-Being and Happiness," Schillebeeckx gives a brilliantly prophetic analysis of the historical circumstances in which we must pick up the threads of apostolic belief and give our own particular witness to Christ as Lord. (I recommend this section of the book as the best *summa theologica* I have read to date!) In a section entitled "Salvation from God: Experienced through Humans and the World," Schillebeeckx examines the famous passage from Genesis concerning the reconciliation of Jacob and Esau, and Jacob's lonely all-night wrestling match with the messenger from God.

To understand this passage, we must put it back into its scriptural context. After having served his uncle Laban for many years, Jacob is returning to his homeland. There he will meet his brother Esau, whom he had fraudulently deprived of his birthright as the firstborn son. The severity of Jacob's sin strikes him; he has sinned not only against Esau, his brother, but also against God. As the meeting nears, Jacob's anxiety grows, and he hears that Esau is coming to meet him with 400 armed men. At this point we become involved in a double story. The first has to do with Jacob's inner struggle with his fears, and the second with his meeting with Esau.

We are first told of the religious and psychological depths of Jacob's laborious attempt at reconciliation with Esau. After wrestling all night with his fears, Jacob succeeds in finding harmony with God and with himself. As a result, his name, Jacob, which means sycophant or self-seeking flatterer, is changed to Israel, which means someone who has come to terms with both God and himself through a laborious inner struggle. The story even has an authentic psychosomatic element in Jacob's dislocated hip, which might have provided him with an excuse to avoid the meeting, and reveals his ambivalence about going through with the reconciliation. But at dawn, Jacob, now Israel, finds the strength and courage to limp across the stream to meet his brother.

Jacob fearfully divides up his flocks and his slaves and sends them off. With fear and trembling, he limps into the camp of Esau and his 400 armed men, sending ahead many gifts to make clear his friendly intention. But when they finally come face to face, Esau drops his war ax and "ran to meet him, took him in his arms and held him close and wept" (Gn. 33:4).

Schillebeeckx finds the pearl of the whole story in verse 10 of chapter 33, where Jacob says to Esau: "To speak truly, I came into your presence as into the presence of God, but you have received me kindly." This verse combines the two stories into a unity. In the forgiveness and acceptance of Jacob and Esau's meeting, God's countenance shines forth like a radiant sun that rises in splendor after a long, troubled night. So too God's countenance shines on all reconciled humans. Those who have been reconciled have a right to live; reconciliation makes our lives worth living, despite all the suffering and injustice we have endured.

This biblical story illustrates two basic themes of Schillebeeckx's theology. The first is that grace comes into our lives with "mediated immediacy." God is directly present to us in worldly things and historical events, even though we may not be aware of that presence. We shall, indeed, be surprised when God says to us: "I was hungry and you fed me!" God reaches us directly, but we reach God only indirectly.

Second, the story illustrates that all efforts to overcome alienation and suffering are at bottom religious strivings that demand God's grace. Christian salvation, God's redemption of us, is connected with the integrity of human life, with being whole—the original meaning of the word *holy*. Thus salvation is concerned with everything that makes human life fully human. In the words of Saint Augustine, to vitiate in any way human self-realization is to vitiate the perfection of God's power. As a result, salvation cannot be sought exclusively in one dimension. It cannot be found solely in moral precepts or in personal mystical experiences. Nor can it be found in an exclusive commitment to political or social reform. All of these are essential dimensions of salvation.

For Jesus, the universality of the saving nearness of God was made present through a life of care for all of his fellow humans, through a selfless championing of suffering humanity. For Jesus, all human suffering was contrary to God's plan. God and suffering are diametrically opposed, and God always seeks to remove it. The only redemptive suffering is that which is voluntarily undertaken or accepted in the effort to liberate others. Any suffering that we impose on each other is anathema. Evidently, Jesus was little interested whether the suffering was the consequence of sin or was innocent. Neither piety nor its lack set any limits to his concern. In his ministry, Jesus saw the sufferings of others as his task; his mission in life was to do all he could to bring relief.

This understanding gives us a norm, a litmus test, to judge whether aspects of Christian practice are in conformity with the spirit of Christ. Whatever aspects of Christian practice contradict the demands of a personal and collective human liberation must be rejected in the name of Christian faith itself. As followers of Jesus, we are obliged by our faith to be active in shaping justice and peace in our society.

At its best the lesbian and gay community has always been an open, democratic community. Gays have frequently succeeded in reconciling differences and in breaking down the barriers that tend to separate us from each other—barriers based on sex, race, class, nationality, or economic status. The most successful gay and lesbian retreats in which I have taken part were those where we faced and dealt with the unconscious prejudice and fears that divided us from each other: lesbian women from gay men, whites from blacks, those who were sexually free from those who were not.

Saint Paul tells us that the work of the Holy Spirit in the world is to gradually break down all the divisions that separate one group of humans from another. He specifically mentions three such divisions: master versus slave, Jew versus Greek, and male versus female. I feel certain that a primary reason why the gay and lesbian community has emerged at this point in history is that it has a special role to play in reconciling the many divisions that plague society, especially those based on the inequality of male and female.

Theology, then, must be constructed from the center of human life, which manifests itself in a history of human emancipation and growth in freedom. Christian freedom and redemption must necessarily be directed toward political and social liberation. If we are to be true to our calling, we must participate in the great liberation movements of our age: in the economic liberation of the poor, especially in the third world; in women's liberation to a status of equality with men; and in gay liberation. We must remember that anything outside us with which we are not reconciled represents a dimension of ourselves with which we are not in harmony.

Schillebeeckx sees certain political consequences flowing from this theological understanding of Christian faith. Our faith does not commit us to any particular political party or program. However, as true followers of Jesus Christ, we are obliged by our faith to be active in shaping justice and peace in our society:

> Through their specific political choice, even if this is through neutrality, Christians may not be party to a political system in which structural or personal compulsion sacrifices the weaker, and injustice becomes a permanent state. Christianity is concerned with the progressive liberation of all humanity. In the light of the gospel, Christians must be partisans and advocates of the poor, those without rights, those who have no representatives anywhere.[2]

Because the gospel summons us to show solidarity with the historical process of human liberation, it is incumbent on us to support those political movements that seek to remove all discrimination, oppression, and personal and institutional exploitation from the world. How far from this understanding was the Vatican letter calling on all the bishops of the world to oppose any legislation granting gay and lesbian people their civil rights!

We can do much toward the healing of humanity, but we are still constantly confronted with human suffering: suffering that results from love; suffering as a result of guilt; suffering that comes from our finitude and mortality; suffering through failure and inadequacy; and, finally, the suffering we experience because of the invisibility and hiddenness of God. No purely human technique of healing can ever totally remove or diminish these sufferings. However, if we can find another human who will freely give up his or her peace and joy in order to descend with us into our private hell of powerlessness, pain, despair, and grief, then we are not alone and there is ground for hope.

Consequently, in every age, the true disciple of Jesus will be committed to removing the causes of human suffering. Every follower of Christ is called to a healing ministry. We are called to recognize the suffering of our times in our own hearts, especially that of our lesbian sisters and gay brothers, and to make that recognition the starting point of our service. This service will not be authentic unless it comes from a heart wounded by the sufferings it seeks to heal. Our healing ministry demands a deep understanding of the ways we can wrestle with God, of how we can courageously overcome our fears in order to make ourselves available as wounded healers.

The AIDS epidemic has provided us in the gay community with the challenge of reconciling all the political differences between us, of overcoming our fears and selfishness in order to collaborate in the task of tending the needs of those who are suffering. For mortal humans, there is no greater achievement than to collaborate in the partial success of human history by making our contribution to the removal of causes of human suffering, wherever that lies within our power. We must remember that heaven takes shape from what we on earth can achieve toward the liberation and salvation of our fellow human beings.

God, our Mother and Father, make us your instrument of reconciliation. Help us to wrestle with all our fears and overcome them so that we may have the courage to seek reconciliation whenever and wherever possible. Amen.

Part Four

The Gay Virtues

Introduction: Hospitality and the Sodom Myth

Those opposed to gay and lesbian rights frequently cite Genesis 19, the story of Sodom and Gomorrah, in support of their position. The history of the interpretation of this passage epitomizes how prejudice and homophobia have distorted the message of Scripture. Throughout the Old and New Testaments, the sin of Sodom was never understood as homosexuality, but rather as selfishness, pride, neglect of the poor, and inhospitality to strangers.

In *The Church and the Homosexual,*[1] I traced the historical process by which a biblical condemnation of inhospitality was transformed into a condemnation of homosexuality. Here is one of the supreme ironies of history: for thousands of years in the Christian West, homosexuals have been victims of, to say the least, inhospitable treatment—the true crime of Sodom—in the name of a mistaken understanding of Sodom's crime. That misunderstanding has traditionally focused on a subtheme of the Sodom story, namely, the practice in ancient Near Eastern religions of depersonalized sex to ensure the fertility of the soil and secure the gods' blessings. This aspect of the Sodom story was confused with the episode's central, positive theme: that God blesses those who are hospitable to strangers.

In a 1986 U.S. Supreme Court decision, Justice Byron White in the majority opinion accepted the state of Georgia's argument that sodomy laws outlawing homosexual activity can be justified by the need to protect morality. Chief Justice Warren Burger concurred with Justice White that "to hold that the act of homosexual sodomy is somehow protected as a fundamental right would be to cast aside millennia of moral teaching."[2]

Inhospitality and the violation of guests' rights, the true crimes of Sodom and Gomorrah, are repeated with impunity by individuals and nations every day. The true sodomites are those who "live in pride and plenty and thoughtless ease, neglect the poor," are inhospitable to refugees, and persecute those who, like Lot and Abraham, offer them sanctuary. I agree with the Supreme Court: they deserve twenty years in prison. What the justices were asked to cast aside was not "millennia of moral teaching" but millennia of homophobia.

In this part, I will deal with what I call the gay virtues: hospitality and compassion. The gay and lesbian community, in spite of the injustice and persecution it has suffered, has always been especially blessed with the virtues of hospitality and compassion. These are, in God's eyes, the virtues that characterized Jesus, and they should be the principal virtues of a follower of Jesus.

In every age, whenever there was a plague, special religious orders of men and women came into existence to take care of the victims. Saint Aloysius Gonzaga, for example, died at the age of twenty-three while ministering to plague victims. In our day, thousands of gay and lesbian volunteers are working with persons with AIDS. Once again, as throughout the history of Western Christianity, it is the gay and lesbian community that is exemplifying these central virtues of Christian life in a striking way.

I want to avoid a possible misunderstanding here. I do want to assert and celebrate what I have experienced clearly as the special gifts and graces that God has poured out on the lesbian and gay community. We read in 1 Peter 4:10: "Each one of you has received a special grace, so, like good stewards responsible for all these different graces of God, put yourselves at the service of others."

In Christian tradition these special graces are given not only to individuals but to groups as well and are connected profoundly to the kind of suffering that group has endured. For example, in his book *We Drink from Our Own Wells*,[3] Gustavo Gutierrez talks about the special graces that arise from the suffering of the poor. I argue in a similar vein that hospitality and compassion are frequently present in a striking way as special gifts arising from the suffering of the lesbian and gay community. I am not claiming that every gay man or lesbian woman manifests these spiritual gifts; on the contrary, many gays and lesbians react with self-pity and cynicism to their exiled state and become extremely selfish. Nor am I claiming that lesbians and gays are better than everyone else. Anyone who develops a mature spiritual life will receive their share of the virtues of compassion and hospitality. Thank God for the thousands of straight doctors, nurses, social workers, ministers, priests, sisters, and lay people who are involved in loving and compassionate service to persons with AIDS. All too often, however, because gay people are for the most part closeted in their public life, their special gifts go unnoticed and unsung.

When I speak of "gay" virtues, I wish to portray the gay and lesbian community as part of a larger "community of virtue" which includes everyone, gay or straight, who seeks to practice the virtues of hospitality and compassion.

11

The Spirit of Hospitality

He came to Nazareth, where he had been brought up, and went into the synagogue on the sabbath day as he usually did. He stood up to read and they handed him the scroll of the prophet Isaiah. Unrolling the scroll he found the place where it is written: "The spirit of the Lord has been given to me, for he has anointed me. He has sent me to bring the good news to the poor, to proclaim liberty to captives and to the blind new sight, to set the downtrodden free, to proclaim the Lord's year of favor." He then rolled up the scroll, gave it back to the assistant and sat down. And all eyes in the synagogue were fixed on him. Then he began to speak to them, "This text is being fulfilled today even as you listen."

Luke 4:16–21

I would like to reflect on the role of the biblical virtue of hospitality in our lives as gay and lesbian Christians and in the context of gay pride. Hospitality is a central virtue in both the Old and New Testaments. One of God's central commandments to Moses on Mount Sinai was: "You must not molest the stranger or oppress him, for you lived as strangers in the land of Egypt" (Ex. 22:20–21). Again, in chapter 18 of Genesis the special quality of Abraham as a good and holy man is dramatically established by his hospitality to strangers. While he is sitting in front of his tent he sees strangers passing in the desert; he rushes out and begs them to enter his tent. He gives them water, washes their feet, and provides a meal for them. (It should be noted that, in the desert, this kind of hospitality could be a question of life or death.)

Similarly, when the angelic strangers push on to Sodom, Lot's standing as a good man worthy of God's favor—in contrast to the other inhabitants of Sodom—is confirmed by his hospitality to the strangers. He insists on inviting them into his house, where he provides them with food and lodging. The primary message of the story of Sodom is that God will bless those who are kind and hospitable to strangers—not that homosexual practices are sinful. The prophet Ezekiel makes clear what the true sin of Sodom was: "The crime of your sister Sodom was pride, gluttony, arrogance, complacency; such were the sins of Sodom and her daughters. They never helped the poor and the needy . . ." (16:48–50). The biblical message concerning human sexuality is that God's gift of sex is to be used for human purposes—it is not to be used as part of divine worship, especially where that involves the abuse and rape of strangers or negates the personal, loving context of sexuality.

Hospitality is also a central theme of the New Testament. For example, Jesus tells his disciples: "And if anyone does not welcome you or listen to what you have to say, as you walk out of the house or town shake the dust from your feet. I tell you solemnly, on the day of Judgment it will not go as hard with the land of Sodom and Gomorrah as with that town" (Mt. 10:14–15). This text makes it clear that Jesus understood the crime of Sodom as inhospitality to strangers.

Again, in chapter 10 of Luke, when someone asks Jesus, "Who is my neighbor?" he responds with the parable of the good Samaritan. Today, this parable might be paraphrased as follows: A man was mugged on 42nd Street and left in an alley close to death. A priest and a social worker passed by and saw him but did nothing because they were afraid. Then a transvestite saw him, went into the alley, picked him up, bound up his wounds with her best scarf, called a taxi, and took him to the emergency room of a hospital. The parable would end in the very same way: with Jesus saying, "Go and do the same yourself."

The Gospel of Luke (24:13–35) tells the story of the disciples as they are walking home along the road to Emmaus, deeply depressed after the death of Jesus. They meet a stranger on the

road who interprets the scriptures for them concerning the death
and resurrection of Jesus and thereby lifts their spirits. When
they reach Emmaus, the stranger starts to go on, but the disciples, like Abraham and Lot, press him to accept their hospitality. When they break bread at table they recognize the risen Jesus.
Again, the message here is that we encounter the divine by
reaching out to our neighbor.

The theme of hospitality continued in Christian tradition, as
can be seen in the motto of the first order of monks, the Benedic-
tines: *Hospes venit, Christus venit*—when a guest comes, Christ
comes. It is also present in the ancient myth of Christopher, in
which the stranger whom Christopher carried across the stream
turned into the Christ child. In ancient Ireland every cottage
would leave its door open and place food and drink by the
fireplace and a candle in the window in case a stranger should
pass by and need hospitality. All of this was the Christian response in faith to Christ's words: "in so far as you did this to one
of the least of these brothers [and sisters] of mine, you did it to
me" (Mt. 25:40).

What Is Hospitality?

Hospitality is not just a question of giving a party and inviting
friends into our house (although it certainly includes this, and
gay people know how to throw a wonderful party). Hospitality
is a state of mind and soul. Henri Nouwen defines hospitality as
"that virtue which allows us to break through the narrowness of
our fears and open our home to the stranger with the understanding that salvation comes to us in the form of a tired travel-
ler."[1] To be able to offer hospitality requires that the host feel at
home in her or his house and be able to create a welcoming and
fearless place for the visitor.

As Nouwen points out, the primary condition for true hospitality is that the host have the freedom to pay attention to the
guest. This can be difficult when we are preoccupied with our
own needs, worries, and anxieties. These preoccupations prevent
us from taking distance from ourselves in order to be there for
the other. Instead of allowing the other to be, we seek to manipulate the other to meet our own needs for sexual fulfillment,
affection, sympathy, friendship, popularity, success, understanding, or money.

The good news is that God loves us; God will meet all our needs. It is our awareness of that love, which comes to us through prayer, that frees us in a spirit of gratitude to give unconditional love to each other. Only if we are a people of prayer will we recognize the stranger as Christ. If we ask daily to recognize Christ in every encounter, we will not end up like those people at the Last Judgment who, upon hearing their sentence, cry out in surprise: "When was it, Lord, that I saw you thirsty and refused to give you a drink of water?" Rather, we will find ourselves face to face with an old friend and daily companion.

A word of caution: there is a very real danger facing the gay community at this time, namely, a negative and destructive understanding of gay pride which I believe we are called on to combat. What I mean was illustrated a few years back in an advertisement in the *New York Times*. The ad read as follows:

> Why would a gay magazine buy this $18,000 page in the *New York Times*?
>
> To give you straight talk about the gay consumer. There's an enormous amount of money in the gay market and it's available to smart advertisers in the ADVOCATE.
>
> Who is the ADVOCATE reader?

The ad goes on to identify as the typical gay male a young man of thirty-eight who has an annual income of $45,000, purchased thirty books in one year, consumed $50 in wine a month, spent $1,200 on camera equipment, acquired a $1,700 stereo system, entertained at home or out fourteen times a month, and traveled to five cities across the country. His education includes two degrees and graduate school. He frequents a gym, plays a Yamaha CS-50 music synthesizer, and composes on his Knabe piano.

There is nothing intrinsically wrong with affluence; the Good Samaritan must have been an affluent man. There is, however, a danger that we gay people, who have been falsely accused of the sin of Sodom, might at the very moment of our liberation become guilty of the real sin of Sodom: the sin of inhospitality and neglect of the poor.

Positive gay pride is pride in our sense of hospitality and compassion. It is too bad that that *New York Times* ad did not go on to mention gay peoples' contributions to charity or their time spent in volunteer service. In my travels around the country and abroad I have been profoundly impressed by the enormous numbers of gay people who are engaged in and deeply committed to loving, hospitable human service. They include priests, ministers, physicians, psychotherapists, counselors, nurses, teachers, social workers, as well as all those involved with the retarded, the sick, the blind, the poor, street people, drug addicts, prisoners, and all the oppressed and outcast. I have been doubly impressed by the extraordinary outpouring of love on the part of the gay community to all the victims of AIDS, an outpouring which is one of the greatest manifestations of hospitable love in our day.

Since most lesbians and gay men do not have children of their own, they tend to redirect a vast reservoir of unselfish love into the human community. So great is that reservoir that the world could not bear its loss. Despite their personal suffering, the loving presence of lesbian women and gay men is the oil that keeps the whole human machine running. If, somehow, gay people were to disappear from the scene, the whole human community would be in danger of being seriously dehumanized.

We gay and lesbian Christians must always remember that dignity is a gift from God, who created us in her own image. Although it is a gift we cannot give ourselves, with God's grace it is one we can give each other. Listen to the words of the prophet Isaiah: "For Yahweh says this: To the eunuchs [i.e., sexual outcasts] who observe my sabbaths, and resolve to do what pleases me and cling to my covenant, I will give, in my house and within my walls, a monument and a name better than sons and daughters; I will give them an everlasting name that shall never be effaced. . . . These I will bring to my holy mountain. I will make them joyful in my house of prayer" (56:4–5).

Almighty God, deepen our awareness of your love for us, your lesbian daughters and gay sons, that, freed from all cynicism and selfishness, we may be present in a compassionate way to every fellow human who is suffering and in need. Amen.

12

The Virtue of Compassion

I want those you have given me to be with me where I am, so that they may always see the glory you have given me because you loved me.

John 17:24

The Sunday between Jesus' ascension into heaven and Pentecost Sunday, when God descended upon the apostles in the person of the Holy Spirit, is a singular Sunday in the liturgical cycle. On this Sunday, the apostles were still in the closet, so to speak, still in the upper room, afraid to come out and reveal their identity as followers of Christ. The apostles spent that time pondering the meaning of Christ's life and how they could be faithful followers of his example. What did they have to do to be able "to see the glory of the Lord"?

I propose that we do the same thing: to look at Christ's life and try to capture the most fundamental spiritual meaning of that life. Let us try to discover how we as his lesbian and gay disciples can struggle to reproduce that spiritual meaning in our lives.

I think that if any one quality sums up the spiritual meaning of Christ's life, that quality is compassion. Saint Paul expressed the compassionate nature of Christ's life beautifully in these words from Philippians:

In your minds you must be the same as Christ Jesus.

His state was divine,
yet he did not cling
to his equality with God
but emptied himself
to assume the condition of a slave,
and became as [humans] are,
and being as all [humans] are,
he was humbler yet,
even to accepting death,
death on a cross.
But God raised him high
and gave him the name
which is above all other names
so that . . .
every tongue should acclaim
Jesus Christ as Lord,
to the glory of God the Father. (2:6–11)

This hymn is a celebration of God's compassion toward us humans, expressed in the life and death of Jesus. Jesus is the greatest human who ever lived precisely because of *his* compassion. The literal meaning of the word compassion is "to suffer along with." Compassion or empathy indicates a free, voluntary process of entering into the sufferings of others in order to liberate them from their suffering. Jesus attained his glory by a process of emptying himself out (*kenosis*). By means of a free empathetic identity with the alienation, loneliness, suffering, and death of his fellow humans, he began the process of healing and liberating them.

Consequently, as followers of Christ we are all called on to be compassionate healers of our fellow human beings. Paul begins his hymn by challenging us: to have the same attitude as Christ. As with hospitality, the primary difficulty we encounter in trying to be compassionate is a preoccupation with our own needs. Instead of acting compassionately toward others, we either ignore them or seek to manipulate them for our own ends.

The spiritual virtue of compassion builds on a special quality of human nature. Psychotherapists recognize that "innate among humans' most powerful striving toward their fellow humans, even in the earliest moments of life, is an essential psychotherapeutic striving, a striving to be a healing influence."[1] In fact, these therapists believe that one of the primary causes of emotional illness is the frustration of that striving to heal: the mentally ill patient is one "whose own ego wholeness is sacrificed throughout life in a truly selfless devotion to complementing the ego-incompleteness of the mothering person."[2] Granting the validity of this insight, and my own professional experience has shown me that it has a great deal of validity, it places most psychological illness in the context and at the service of a redemptive love.

Certain conditions are necessary for one to undertake a Christian healing ministry, which is something that every follower of Christ is called to in her or his own way. The Christian healer is one who is willing to put his or her articulated faith at the disposal of those who ask for help. By articulation I mean that the Christian healer must have undergone some degree of self-analysis, similar to that practiced by secular therapists, who must go through analysis so that their unconscious will not get in the way of the therapy.

First, Christian healers must have wrestled inwardly with temptation, despair, and the dark night of the soul. They must bring all their anger into full consciousness so they are fully aware of their anger at parents, at the church, and at God. They must also have dealt with all the fear and guilt in their unconscious, especially fear of death and fear of God, lest they collude with the person they are trying to help in avoiding painful issues whose resolution is essential to spiritual growth and peace. They should be able to articulate the movements of the interior life and identify their spiritual experiences, so that they are no longer victims of their unconscious and will be able slowly and consistently to remove all the obstacles that prevent the Spirit from entering.

Second, a follower of Christ's healing mission must be a person of compassion. In fact, compassion must become the core and even the nature of his or her authority. There is a serious danger here, especially for those of us professionally involved in ministry and in healing: we are in danger of becoming proud of our competence and human skills, and we may be tempted to use our professional status as an excuse to avoid the much more difficult task of being compassionate. Our skillful diagnostic eye may become more the eye of a distant, detached analyst than the eye of a compassionate partner.

Precisely because Jesus freely emptied himself and took on our human condition, we humans have the power, in his name, to lead our fellow humans to freedom. However, no one can help another on the spiritual level without having the spiritual freedom to enter with his or her whole being into the painful situation. One must also take the risk of being wounded and even destroyed in the process.

The great fallacy of Christian leadership is to think that you can lead someone out of the spiritual desert of depression, hopelessness, and despair without having been there yourself. We are all called to recognize the sufferings of our brothers and sisters, especially our gay brothers and sisters, in our own hearts and make that recognition the starting point of our service. In other words, we are called to be "wounded healers." One of the great joys of Christian life is the discovery that we can make our own wounds available as a resource for the healing of others. In the proclamation of the Easter Vigil we sing, "O felix culpa, O happy fault, O necessary sin of Adam which gained us so great a redeemer!" God takes our deepest wounds, failings, and sinfulness and transforms them into a powerful means of helping others. Anyone who has been a member of Alcoholics Anonymous knows exactly how this works.

A compassionate person can comfort a despairing neighbor only by giving up the comfort of his or her own hope and faith and by entering empathetically into the neighbor's despair. If anyone is willing to enter into my private hell and stay there with me, then there are grounds for hope. Jesus cried out in agony in the garden of Gethsemane: "My soul is sorrowful to the point of death. Wait here and keep awake with me" (Mt. 26:38). That cry for human companionship still echoes in our ears. It is precisely in that moment of utter powerlessness that God's power will be revealed.

By sharing our pain and suffering, we can help each other become more firmly aware that suffering and death have lost their final claim on us. Because of the mercy and compassion of our savior, Jesus Christ, the last word is that of Easter Sunday— a word of eternal life and love. Our God, who revealed him/ herself in the humble and broken body of Jesus on the cross, continues to reveal his/her presence whenever and wherever human suffering becomes visible.

The following news item illustrates how one modern-day

cleric's exercise of compassion got him into trouble. In 1987 Archbishop Raymond G. Hunthausen was relieved of his duties as archbishop of Seattle because of, among other things, his compassionate pastoral stance toward the lesbian and gay community. The *New York Times* reported on May 27, 1987, that a commission of three Roman Catholic bishops named to assess the situation issued a report to the Holy See that contained this statement:

> The Archbishop attributes a great value to *compassion*. His own practice of compassion has become legendary. While the Archbishop himself, however, seems generally to balance compassion with the law, and asserts unconditionally his own commitment to formal Church teaching, it seems that some who admire his compassion may not give similar weight to the place and demands of the law, bending it in important matters under the aegis of compassion.

The commission recommended that the archbishop should recover his authority as diocesan bishop, but only under the condition that he temper compassion with law.

Compassion is a universal religious value. While I was praying over my orders from the Vatican, a monk at the Abbey of Gethsemane called my attention to a Buddhist text, *The Bodhisattva's Vow of Universal Redemption*. He explained to me that a Bodhisattva is one who, after attaining enlightenment, defers his or her entrance into nirvana (that is, cessation of the cycle of birth and death) and chooses instead to continue being born in a human body in order to share the burden of others' sufferings and sorrows and to aid them by his or her compassionate presence. Sharing the suffering of the human state, the Bodhisattva freely chooses "exile" until all human beings can enter into salvation. The vow reads:

> I take upon myself the burden of my suffering brothers [and sisters], I am resolved to do so, I will endure it, I will not turn or run away, I will not turn back. I cannot.
>
> And why? My endeavors do not merely aim at my own deliverance. I must help all my brothers [and sisters] cross the stream of this life which is so difficult to cross. With the help of the boat of compassion I must help them across the stream.

I would fain become a soother of all the sorrows of my brothers [and sisters]. May I be a balm to those who are sick, their healer and servant until sickness come never again. May I become an unfailing store for my poor brothers [and sisters] and serve them in their need. May I be in the famine of the ages' end their drink and meat.

My own being, all my life, all my spirituality in the past, present and future I surrender that my brothers [and sisters] may win through to their end, for they dwell in my spirit.

The spirit of this vow is exactly the spirit being lived out by thousands of gay and lesbian people as well as many others who have dedicated themselves as volunteers to do whatever they can to relieve the suffering of persons with AIDS.

A word of caution is in order at this point. There are pathological as well as healthy forms of compassion and empathy. The pathological forms are the principal cause of the phenomenon known as burn-out. Pathological compassion, such as Searles describes in his patients, is based on a masochistic form of symbiosis, a loss of or failure to achieve ego identity and ego boundaries, which results in a sense of fusion with the other. For example, there have been times when I have become too fused with a depressed client, with the result that the client left the session relatively freed from depression while I continued to feel depressed for hours afterward. Healthy compassion is based on a clear, separate identity of the self and the ability to maintain clear ego boundaries.

Although compassionate persons give up the *comfort* of their faith and hope in order to share the feelings of hopelessness and despair of others, they do not give up their faith and hope themselves. A clear awareness of this distinction and the ability to practice it is also necessary to avoid burn-out. This warning is especially important to people who work with persons with AIDS.

In her book *Prisoners of Childhood*,[3] Alice Miller points out that many people involved in healing, such as ministers or counselors, are skilled in empathy because they themselves had narcissistic mothers. Thus from earliest childhood they developed special antennae that allowed them to tune in and respond to their mothers' needs while denying and repressing their own needs. These people lack a healthy narcissism; unconscious rage at the repression and denial of their own needs accompanies their empathetic responses. Such people, Miller claims, can make excellent therapists or counselors, but only if they can learn how to meet their own needs in a healthy way and not bring unconscious frustration and rage into their work. Again, it is this frustration and rage that frequently underlie burn-out.

In my own practice I have found myself to be a wounded healer. Frequently I have fallen short of the spiritual ideal of compassion. As a young man in a prisoner-of-war camp in Germany during World War II, I fantasized about my future ministry in terms of embracing a dying soldier and absorbing his pain into my body so that he could die in peace. Since then I have been blessed on many occasions to be able to play such a role. Frequently, however, someone in mortal pain has called me and I have been unwilling or unable to reach out and embrace them. I have had to go through a painful process of recognizing my limits.

The ideal for a follower of Christ, however, remains perfectly clear: our attitude must be Christ's own attitude, namely, one of compassion. May God grant us all the strength to grow toward that ideal. We should always remember Christ's words to Mary Magdalene after her compassionate gesture of washing his feet with her tears and drying them with her hair: "Her many sins must have been forgiven her, or she would not have shown such great love" (Lk. 7:47). One gesture of compassion can wipe out a whole lifetime of sins.

Compassion, like hospitality, is a virtue extraordinarily alive in the gay community. Gay people are involved in compassionate works of human service out of all proportion to their numbers in the community. The world has noted the recent astonishing outpouring of compassion by lesbians and gay men to all persons with AIDS. (We will explore later the reasons for this exceptional spiritual development in the gay community.) With the AIDS crisis, gay love and gay compassion have come out of the closet, and the world is saying: See how they love one another!

I would like to close this reflection on compassion with these words from the Gospel of Luke: "Be compassionate as your Father is compassionate. Do not judge, and you will not be judged yourselves; do not condemn, and you will not be condemned yourselves. Give, and there will be gifts for you: a full measure, pressed down, shaken together, and running over, will be poured into your lap; because the amount you measure out is the amount you will be given back" (Lk. 6:36–38). At the heart of Christian life is a mysticism of compassion. It is this that will reveal to us God's power and presence.

Almighty God, because of your loving compassion for us, our lives are full of joy and hope. Help us in turn to be compassionate to each other out of a spirit of love for our brothers and sisters and a spirit of sincere gratitude to you. Amen.

Part Five

Celebrating Life

Introduction: The Freedom to Play

I have come so that they may have life and have it to the full.

John 10:10

Lesbians and gays are extraordinarily gifted as celebrants of life. A high proportion of human creative genius has traditionally come from within the gay and lesbian community. Our Steins, Sapphos, Adrienne Riches, da Vincis, Michelangelos, and Shakespeares have tended to be gay or lesbian. At the heart of all true creativity lies the freedom to play. The first chapter in this part deals with the conditions that make possible a life lived as play.

The most important arena for human playfulness that God has created is sexuality. As in every other area of human life, the work ethic has taken over and sex has tended to become another form of work. Chapter 14, entitled "This Is My Body," explores the interplay between the spiritual significance of our bodies and their erotic dimension, along with the fundamental role the body plays in our spiritual life. Chapter 15, on sexuality as play, explores God's intentions for our human sexuality, the possibility of restoring playfulness to sex, and the important role the gay community has played in that restoration.

We have already noted the special role a mother's love plays in freeing a child to play. In chapter 16 we will deal with the special role that Mary, the mother of God, played in my life by making God's maternal love for me concrete and freeing me to turn life into play.

13

The Freedom to Play

Sing out with a voice of joy; let it be heard to the ends of the earth. The Lord has set his people free! Alleluia!

Collect for Easter Sunday

In the Gospels, liberation is always a sign of the presence of the Holy Spirit, the spirit of love and the spirit of Christ. Wherever and whenever true human liberation occurs, we can be certain of the presence and activity of the Spirit. "You will be able to tell them by their fruits" (Mt. 7:16). (A biblical statement that always makes a gay person smile.) I would like to reflect on one type of human liberation implied in God's gift of his spirit of love— liberation from the "work ethic" so that a spirit of play may take its place.

The Work Ethic

One of the intrinsic features of American culture is the work ethic. The value judgment that accompanies this ethic is that our value as human beings lies in the work we do. We have to earn our value through our work, and that work has frequently been understood in the past, in a very narrow sense, as the production of material goods. The logical conclusion of this kind of thinking is that our moral goodness depends on our willingness to commit ourselves to duty for its own sake in the form of difficult and dehumanizing work. Kant, for example, was convinced that our worst distraction from moral duty was the search for pleasure and happiness.

The work ethic is so much part of our culture and of ourselves that leisure time causes us very real difficulty. The average American feels very guilty when he or she is unemployed or on vacation. Perhaps for a day or two they regard their leisure as valuable because it prepares them to return to work with renewed energy and enthusiasm. But any leisure beyond what is strictly necessary produces deep-seated feelings of uselessness, guilt, and self-condemnation. A dramatic example is the common experience of retired persons who literally lose their will to live once their regular employment in the community is ended.

Perhaps the most dramatic expression of the work ethic in modern history was the directive sent by Emperor Joseph of Belgium in the early 1900s to the administrators of the Belgian territory in the Congo. In this directive, he pointed out that the basis of all civilization was, in his opinion, the spirit of work. Consequently, if he were to fulfill his duty of civilizing the Congo, he must teach the natives the spirit of work. He therefore ordered that that natives be gathered together into work camps, where they would be assigned daily quotas of work, such as gathering so many pounds of latex or laying so many miles of railroad ties. If anyone failed to execute his or her daily quota, drastic penalties were applied, such as the amputation of a hand.

A stark contrast to the emperor's attitude may be seen in the lives of a Pygmy tribe from the rain forest of Africa who were featured in a television documentary. These people rise at dawn and do about an hour's work, such as gathering bananas, preparing meals, and repairing the thatched roofs on their huts, which is all they have to do to obtain the necessities of life. All the rest of the day they play. They hold ceremonial dances and set up contests to see who can swing the farthest on jungle vines. Even grandfathers and grandmothers join the fun. These people's philosophy of life, or rather their theology, involves the belief that they are children of a loving father who enjoys their play. Thus their play is the most important element in their lives. Through joyous play they manifest their gratitude to God for their exis-

tence. If one of them were to become anxious and begin to collect more bananas than he needed for the day and hoard things
and have no time for play, his neighbors would think that he was
sick or had lost his faith and trust in their god.

These are the sort of people whom the Emperor Joseph
thought had to be taught the value of work. But the only way to
do so would be to destroy their theology—their belief that God
loves them for what they are and not for what they do. One
would also have to destroy their psychological health, that is,
their confidence in their self-worth. They would have to learn to
be anxious about their value as people and feel that they must
somehow prove themselves by what they can produce in the way
of practical results through hard work.

Although the work ethic had its origins in Europe, it reached
its full development in American culture, where it fused with the
frontier spirit, native American pragmatism, and American pu-
ritanism. Certainly that ethic served a purpose as long as the
average life span was about thirty-five and we were busy meeting
the challenge of the frontier in our collective effort to built a great
industrial nation. Today, however, the work ethic is running into
a number of inherent contradictions. I believe that these contradictions, which will become progressively more manifest, are all
connected with the cybernetic revolution. For the first time in its
history humanity has the means to turn over most of the real
work of providing food, clothing, and shelter to machines. The
vast majority of new jobs today are in the field of human services.

The primary contradiction, then, lies in the fact that our
psychology is still caught up in the work ethic although the
amount of work we do and the time devoted to it have been and
in all likelihood will continue to be reduced drastically. In my
own lifetime I have witnessed the reduction of the work week
from a ten-hour, six-day week to an eight-hour, five-day week,
and there is the possibility of further reduction. We begin work
much later in life. Some cynics claim that the only reason for
college is to keep young people off the labor market. We retire
much earlier. And we live much longer. As a result, the time we
have for leisure is greatly increased.

I have already indicated the kinds of problem that leisure
time creates for many people. Another contradiction in the work
ethic is that it holds up affluence and leisure as goals in order to

motivate people to work harder, when the very achievement of those goals leads to a sense of loss of personal value and the ostensible reward becomes more of a curse than a blessing. The practice of giving retiring employees a gold watch right at the time when they will least need it seems ironic indeed.

One of the great flaws in the work ethic is that it deprives us of the ability to live in the present moment and renders us victims of the tyranny of time. When one is working, the activity is not meaningful in itself but only in terms of what comes after: the money earned, the leisure or success or prestige gained. One endures the drudgery of the present in hope of what the future will bring.

One's whole life can be caught up in this attitude with the result that the quality of life is destroyed. The high-school student waits for graduation; the college student waits for graduate school; the graduate student waits for a job; the worker waits for a vacation; the vacationer waits to go back to work; the veteran worker waits for retirement. Our whole life can be spent waiting for what comes next. Then death intervenes and in a way it can be said that we never really existed, because we never found time to do something for its own sake; that is to say, we never played.

The fundamental theological myth concerning work in Christian culture is found in Genesis, where the first humans are described as living in the Garden of Eden, in paradise. There, like the Pygmies in the rain forest, they played in the presence of God. But then they sinned, and the curse visited on them because of that sin was a loss of the awareness of God's loving presence. They became anxious and were told: "with sweat on your brow shall you eat your bread" (Gn. 3:19). In other words, the need to work was a result of their sin.

From this viewpoint, the whole history of humanity to the present day can be understood as a progressive effort, based in the blood, sweat, and tears of our ancestors, to liberate us from the curse of work. Today, because of the cybernetic revolution, we stand on the threshold of that day of liberation.

Some theologians interpret the myth of the Garden of Eden as a primordial dream of humanity concerning the goal of all human evolution and development. What was cast in terms of a historical narrative really represents the ideal goal of all human striving. In any case, work was originally understood as a curse based on sin, but the work ethic distorts that curse into a blessing and tries to keep humanity subject to that curse in an age where liberation has become possible.

Another essential aspect of the work ethic is that it leads to the subordination of persons to things. The work ethic demands that we judge our own value on the basis of our productivity. Our relationships with persons are considered secondary and largely irrelevant. Recent political proposals to reform welfare are frequently based on a dramatic appeal to the American work ethic; the welfare system is to be reformed by forcing massive numbers of people back into the job market. I fully support any effort to make jobs available for all those who want and need jobs. But the interesting aspect of the proposed reforms is that the mother on welfare, who stays at home and dedicates herself entirely to her children, to developing their personalities and serving their needs, is not considered to be making a worthwhile contribution to the community because she is not a part of the work force. Some have proposed that welfare mothers be forced to leave the home in order to work and that their children be placed in day care. This same kind of prejudice finds expression in the inferior salaries paid to teachers, nurses, social workers, or others who provide human services but do not work with things. These are also the primary tasks to which gay people feel drawn and by means of which they try to establish their identity and value in the heterosexual community.

Our use of the word "bum" is a very interesting indicator of our implicit value system. A "bum" is someone for whom we have no respect, someone we consider to be valueless. But what is a "bum"? Someone who does not work for a living. The work ethic is also built into our legal system. In most American communities the law stipulates that if you are discovered loitering, do not have a certain sum of money in your pocket, and do not have a job, you are a vagrant. In that case you have no right to be in that community. You are put in jail overnight and the next day you are told to move on.

The subordination of persons to things is built into the very structure of our society. We often hear of one or another American industry demanding the same sort of loyalty from its employees that one would expect from a member of the family. Yet once the individual can no longer make a profitable contribution, industry no longer feels any reciprocal loyalty. How many people have been laid off just one year before they were eligible for a pension? The only family many businesses resemble is the Eskimo family of old, where the day that grandmother's teeth gave out and she could no longer chew the skins, she was put out on an ice shelf and bid a tearful good-bye.

It is instructive to recall the book that at one time was the bible of the aspiring young American businessman, Dale Carnegie's *How to Win Friends and Influence People*. This book should top the list as one of the most immoral books ever written, for what I understand to be its message is that one should pretend genuine interest in other persons, not for their own sake, but in order to use them. This is precisely the meaning of the word hypocrisy. One practices smiling, saying the right thing, and pretending to have the right interests in order to win the other's confidence and make a sale. One's object is to get ahead in life one way or another. This book was written totally within the context of the work ethic.

Gay and lesbian people are particularly susceptible to becoming victims of the work ethic. Having been taught from childhood that their difference is somehow bad and makes them unworthy of love and acceptance, gay people frequently feel that they must out-perform all their peers in order to compensate. Workaholism based on anxiety is a common disease in the gay and lesbian community.

What Is Play?

What, then, is the alternative to the work ethic? The opposite of work is not sloth or inactivity; rather, it is play. Play should be understood as a basic human activity, irreducible to anything else.

Most analysts of play make the mistake of reducing it to a means to something else, and that something is usually work. This is the case with the type of psychological study that attempts to explain children's play-behavior as an instinctual process whereby they learn to cope with reality, a preparatory behavior to work wherein one learns to develop new skills. Play certainly achieves this, but if this were the child's intention the activity would no longer be play.

Because play occupies such an important position in our lives, we would do well to focus our efforts on cultivating the possibility of play within the human community. The first condition necessary for play is that the human activity must be meaningful in itself and not be related to a goal that lies beyond the playful action itself; it must be totally meaningful here and now. A perfect illustration of this quality is the activity of dancing.

This aspect of play also has a close connection with the quality of our interpersonal relationships. If it is impossible for us to live fully in the present moment, then we will never be able to be present fully for another person. The ability to do so and, consequently, the ability to be fully present for another is probably the primary reason why, when we succeed in playing, we experience such intense joy and fulfillment.

As the German poet Schiller put it, "Humans are only fully human when they play." Johan Huizinga, in his classic book *Homo Ludens: A Study of the Play Element in Culture,*[1] sees play as the fullest expression of our humanity because it is the fullest expression of human freedom. Play is an expression of personal initiative and of the self, free from all extrinsic constraint. Huizinga builds a good case for the thesis that all human civilization—commerce, science, law, and all the arts—has its foundation not in work, but in play. Even religious worship is a form of play. In a statement on the meaning and role of liturgy, the American Catholic bishops explained that the purpose of liturgy was "to teach us how to celebrate our existence." Huizinga points out that if play is the foundation of all civilization, to lose the sense of play is to threaten that very foundation.

The gay community has always been a community with an extraordinary freedom to play. Society is keenly aware that creative gay people are represented in the arts—the theater, the plastic arts, music, ballet, film, fashion—out of all proportion to their numbers in the population at large. The incredible loss to the entire human community of creative talent because of the AIDS-related deaths of so many gifted gay men is painful proof of this thesis.

Some of that freedom to play comes, I believe, from the gay community's acceptance of its exiled status. We are frequently no longer involved in competing. As a result, lesbians and gays are much freer to develop an aesthetic sense and to engage in activities for their own sake. Jung attributes the creativity of the gay male community to its ability to be in touch with the feminine as well as the masculine aspects of the self.

In order to clarify further what I mean by play, I must make an important distinction. The very same action can be either work or play. Whether or not one is working or playing depends not so much on what one is doing but on the spirit and the conditions under which one does it. The person, for example, who works in the garden on a weekend may be doing back-breaking work but still be playing.

This leads us to the next condition necessary for an activity to take the form of play. Play always calls into question the type of interpersonal relationship within which the activity takes place. An example of this would be the contrast between the relationship of workers on the job and the relationship of the same people on the company bowling team.

If a person on a bowling team had to earn a certain score in order to make a living, bowling could easily become the worst form of drudgery. But when the game is purely recreational, despite the amount of effort required in the game, the people involved are playing and enjoying themselves. (At least this is usually the case. When competitiveness becomes too intense it can destroy the play quality of any sport.)

In a game such as bowling, it is interesting to note how giving a handicap can change the nature of the bowlers' attitude toward each other. The purpose of the handicap is to allow even the least skilled player to compete on an equal basis with his or her teammates. In this way, the less skilled player achieves a sense of equality and his or her anxiety over success or failure is lessened.

Another curious difference between work and play has to do with the attitude toward cheating. Many young persons who would not hesitate to cheat in an exam, if they thought they could escape detection, would not dream of cheating in a game.

Another key difference between work and play is that the attitude of work is always based in anxiety. Anxiety, the late Bishop Fulton Sheen was fond of saying, is a form of atheism. Frequently, people in industry strive to increase productivity by increasing anxiety concerning job security or pay raises. Play, in contrast, can only take place when there is a felt sense of security. Animals, for example, will engage in playful behavior, but only if they are well-fed and feel safe from their enemies. Psychologists have observed that a seriously disturbed child will cease to play. The only way the disturbed child can be freed to play once again is to give him or her the felt security of being loved. The unconditional love of the mother frees the infant to play. Conditioned love results in pathology, in the feeling that one needs to earn love through work.

Some theologians have argued that adults are free to play only when they become aware that God loves them for their own sake and not for what they do. "What proves that God loves us is that Christ died for us while we were still sinners" (Rm. 5:8). Thus the freedom to be able to play all of life in the presence of a loving God is a central message of revelation. God, our parent in heaven, through the redemption wrought by Jesus Christ, has freed us from the curse of work and created for us once again the freedom to play.

The final and most important condition for play has to do with the type of community within which the activity takes place. There are two basic types of human community: the functional and the personal. In a functional community, the interrelations between persons are not meaningful in themselves but only as a means of productivity of some sort. Authority in a functional community exists in order to coordinate the efforts of the group toward that productivity.

A personal community, such as the family, is quite different. The community is its own end; it is the loving interrelationships between the members that justify the existence of the community. Productivity within the personal community is secondary and has its source in the overflow of the joy and love that unites the members of the community. Authority in a personal community has as its primary task to promote dialogue, to bring about personal interaction and mutual affirmation among the members. The personal community is based on the fact that we need each other. We need others to affirm us in our existence, to make us feel that we mean something and that we have value. We need the security of being loved and giving love in return. It is only to the degree that we find ourselves members of a true personal community that we have the necessary security and confidence to be able to play.

But the true source of the freedom to play is God's unconditional love for us, which we cannot merit and we do not have to earn. As the good news of God's love penetrates our hearts, we are free to be able to love each other unconditionally. It is love that creates the space in which we are free to dance and sing. It is love that frees us all to be able to play. Our only appropriate response to this gift of the freedom to play is gratitude.

I would like to finish this reflection of play with an anecdote from J. D. Salinger's novel *Raise High the Roof Beam, Carpenters*. Salinger recounts a conversation between the young hero of the novel and his older brother, who had just become champion marble player of all Brooklyn. The younger brother asks, "Seymour, what is the secret of your success?" Seymour ponders awhile and answers: "Don't aim!"[2] I believe the whole secret of life is in those two words.

Almighty God, we lesbians and gays are your special children. Give us such a profound experience of your love that, healed of our wounds, we will be free to play our lives in your presence. Amen.

14

This Is My Body

You must love the Lord your God with all your Heart, with all your soul, and with all your mind. This is the greatest and the first commandment. The second resembles it: You must love your neighbor as yourself. On these two commandments hang the whole Law, and the Prophets also.

Matthew 22:37–40

"This is my body." Let us hear again those startling words. Let us see Jesus speak them over the bread, Jesus desiring and willing to be present to us in and through his body until the end of time; Jesus establishing the new covenant by his body and blood so that for all time the meeting place between God and humanity, the means of communication by which we become one with God and God becomes one with us, will be the flesh and blood of Jesus.

I would like to reflect with you on the mystery of the body, both Christ's body and our own.

When as a young man I made my first trip to Chicago, I remember being very impressed by a statue by the French sculptor, Rodin, which at that time was located on a landing of the main staircase in the Art Institute. The statue was hewn from a huge block of granite. Emerging from the stone, but still partially trapped in it, were the bodies of men and women. Each figure was straining every muscle trying to reach around to the figures on either side of it, but none could touch more than the fingertips of the others. The title Rodin had given this masterful work was *The Isolation of the Human Spirit.*

Rodin's statue dramatically expresses the paradox of the human body. It is our body that keeps us apart from each other, allows us to be separate, unique individuals, autonomous and free. Yet that same body is the means by which we communicate and achieve union with each other.

Frequently, we Christians fail to accept our bodies as God intends us to accept them. And failing to accept our own bodies fully, we may fail to fully accept Christ's incarnation and the reality of the Resurrection. Sometimes we unconsciously fall victim to those ancient heresies that, like Manichaeanism, see the body with its sexual drive and hungers as evil and a source of sin. We then are tempted to see ourselves as essentially a soul or spirit housed in a body which we use but with which we are not identified. The corollary of this alienation from our God-given body is the view that human sexuality is something evil, something that drives us away from God. Death thus appears as a welcome release from the prison of the body, and we begin to understand the hereafter in terms of the immortality of the soul instead of the resurrection of the body.

But all this is not the teaching of Christ. On the contrary, it was Plato and the Greek pagan philosophers who taught the immortality of the soul; indeed, they would have judged the Christian message of resurrection to be pure foolishness. Jesus revealed an immortality that is to be achieved by a miraculous resurrection and transformation of the body.

One of the primary reasons for our denial of our bodies is the difficulty we experience with our sexual drive. As we evolve toward spiritual maturity, each of us must struggle with our sexual drive so that, with God's grace, it will cease to be a selfish destructive force and become instead a power integrated into our personality as a means of communicating love.

We have succeeded in integrating another bodily function, eating, to the point where heaven itself is symbolized as a banquet, and the family dinner has been fully integrated into our social and spiritual life. Just as there are prayers before and after a meal, so too there should be prayers before and after sex. To the extent that this idea shocks us, we may gauge the extent to which we remain alienated from our body and its God-given sexuality.

Every effort we make at communication—a handshake; a kiss; using our mouth and lips not for eating, as nature intended, but to produce speech—has a bodily, nongenital sexual component. We are not spirits that use a body; we *are* our body. By the same token, sex is not just something we do; it is an inalienable dimension of what we are.

I would like to address the issue of the interrelationship between love of God and love of our whole selves, including our body. I would also like to explore the connection between fear of God and fear of the erotic dimension of our bodies.

By stating that there is really only one commandment, namely, the commandment to love, Jesus wished to emphasize the special quality of our relationship to God in the new covenant. No longer are we to worship God in a spirit of fear; rather, we are to relate to God as adopted children to a loving parent and not as slaves to a master. We must beware, then, of the kind of fear that can crush out the love of God from our hearts and lead us back into a worship of fear, in a sort of post-Christian paganism.

Notice that Jesus' first commandment orders us to love God with all our heart. In the New Testament, the heart is a symbol for the body and its feelings. We are exhorted to let the love of God penetrate our whole being, including the body and all its feelings. This implies that there is a sensuous and even erotic dimension to our love of God, a dimension so essential to our ability to love as embodied humans that to deny it would cripple our spiritual life as well.

I am reminded of a sermon Saint Augustine once gave to a community of celibate women in Hippo. Commenting on the biblical parable of the Wise and Foolish Virgins, Augustine made the point that chastity in itself does not get anyone into heaven. Both the wise and the foolish virgins were chaste, but only the wise virgins who had "oil in their lamps" were allowed into the wedding feast when the bridegroom arrived. What, Augustine asked, does oil in their lamps signify? His answer was that the oil in the lamps of the wise virgins signified their ability to express warm human love, whereas the foolish virgins were cold and distant, expecting to get into heaven because of their moralistic perfectionism. Augustine was making the point that there is a pathological as well as a healthy form of chastity. But in the end, there is only one way to gain admittance to the heavenly banquet, and that is through love.

Jesus goes on to tell us that the second part of his commandment is identical (*homoia*) to the first, that is, the commandment to love God is the same as the commandment to love our neighbor as ourselves. This identity is so strong that John feels free to say that if anyone claims to love God and nevertheless hates their neighbor, that person is a liar (1 Jn. 4:20).

At a lesbian and gay rights dinner,[1] Rita Mae Brown quoted with approval a saying of her mother: "God loves me through my friends." For most of us, love of God remains an abstraction, an idea to which nothing real corresponds, unless that love can be incarnated into our lives. Just as Jesus is the incarnation of God's love for us, so too most of us come through to a belief and trust in God's love through our experience of human love—the love of a parent, friend, partner or through a loving community.

I would like to focus on the third dimension of Jesus' commandment: love of self. Jesus tells us that we shall love our neighbor *as* ourselves. A certain healthy narcissism is implied here. Love begins with oneself. Many have misinterpreted this commandment as saying: You shall love your neighbor *more* than yourself. Some even seem to think it means that you shall love your neighbor and *hate* yourself. These people replace a healthy narcissism with masochism, and believe that they are glorifying God through self-rejection and self-hatred.[2] I would even extend John's statement and add that those who claim they love their neighbor and hate themselves are liars.

The first and greatest commandment presupposes that all three loves—love of self, neighbor, and God—are all of a piece. If one is missing, then the others cannot exist. Which brings us back to our body once again. I believe that the most profound and most frequent sin concerning our bodies and their erotic dimension has nothing to do with sexual activity. On the contrary, it has to do with our alienation from our body and its sexual feelings and our effort to reject or repress the erotic dimension of our being, an effort that represents a refusal of God's good gift of sexuality and a distrust of creation.

All alienation from God's good creation is the result of sin, and alienation from our bodies is depicted in Scripture as the root of sin. We read in Genesis that our first parents, Adam and Eve, were perfectly at home with themselves, their bodies, and with God until they sinned. It was only then that they became alienated from and ashamed of their nakedness. As a consequence of this alienation from their bodies, they also became alienated from each other and from God. Love of neighbor disappeared, and Cain even went so far as to slay his brother. Humanity had lost the reality of the loving presence of God.

In a work entitled *The Feast of Love,* Pope John Paul II, writing from a traditional heterosexist, dualistic perspective, sees the sin of Adam and Eve as "lustful activity." After the harmony between God and humanity had been broken, the lower (i.e., sexual) nature of human beings no longer obeyed the higher. Sebastian Moore, in a masterful critique of this book,[3] points out that, three different times, the author of Genesis identifies Adam and Eve's sin not as lustful activity, but rather as willful alienation from their body and its sexual feelings.

For Adam and Eve, the body became for them an object over against the self, something to be constrained out of fear or to be indulged as a source of pleasure. Either way, the alienated body is divorced from the spiritual self. Both these extremes miss the point that God intends sexual wholeness to be a part of our redemption.

If every human being experiences a certain degree of alienation from his or her body and its sexual feelings, how much more alienated can lesbians and gay men become if they accept the view that their sexual orientation is an objective disorder, a tendency to evil, and a defect in creation. And how much harder is the struggle gay people must undergo to accept themselves and their sexuality.

In my work as a psychotherapist I have become aware how many people, in an effort to repress their sexual feelings, crush out all feeling whatsoever and live lives devoid of warmth and intimacy. There is also a connection between alienation from the body and the depersonalization of sex. The unloving suppression of the self's erotic needs frequently leads to the destructive acting out of those needs. What we reject in ourselves, we tend to project outward: sexism, heterosexism, homophobia, hatred of women or hatred of men, racism.

It has always been the prophetic role of lesbians and gay men to lead the church and Western culture toward reembracing embodiment, toward a sense of identity with the body and its sensuousness. We must let our "word become flesh." This is the message of the lesbian and gay community. We must give up our dualistic, escapist concept of being immortal souls encased in a mortal body that we use but are not identified with. We must learn how to live in, enjoy, and celebrate our bodies with gratitude to God.

Paradoxically, Christianity, which has been so antisexual in practice, differs from other world religions in having a positive attitude toward the human body. Christian revelation contains at least four essential affirmations of the body, including its sexual dimension.

The first is the biblical account of creation. In the second chapter of Genesis, which is the original creation narrative, predating the first chapter by over 500 years, God announces, "It is not good that the man should be alone. I will make him a helpmate" (2:18). The first human couple was thus united by a sexual bond. The same theme is taken up in the Song of Songs, an entire book of the Bible given over to a grateful celebration of God's gift of erotic love.

The second affirmation of the body is the Incarnation. As the Gospel of John tells us, "the Word was made flesh and lived among us" (Jn. 1:14). Jesus was a sexual being; he underwent circumcision. If Jesus accepted and rejoiced in an embodied, sexual existence, then we too should let our word become flesh; we should be able to accept and rejoice in our sexual bodies.

The third affirmation is the establishment of the Eucharist as Christ's memorial: "This is my body." Christ could have chosen to be with us for all time through his spirit alone, but he chose to be with us through his human body as well.

The fourth is the Resurrection. We do not share the pagan concept of eternal life as a life only of the spirit, with the body serving merely as a temporary shell to be discarded. In some way, our flesh will be part of our identity for all eternity.

We can only get to heaven in and through our sexual, mortal body. Therefore we must do battle with and overcome our alienation from our body and its sexuality. This is a dimension of our salvation and one of the healing graces Jesus won for us. Adam and Eve, by wanting to become like God, grew ashamed of their sexual bodies. Jesus, on the other hand, who was the "Word of God," *became* flesh. And because the Word became flesh, we can allow *our* word to become flesh; we can overcome all alienation from our body and accept our identity with it. We must trust that our Creator so designed the self's erotic nature that it is intrinsically aimed, not at an impersonal sexual hedonism, but at personal sexual communion. Thus our task is, with the help of God's grace, to integrate that sexual nature into our power to love—to love ourselves, to love each other and ultimately to love God with our whole being. Even our compulsive, promiscuous sexual activity is a flawed search for unity with each other and with God. A word of peace, encouragement, and hope to all those who are finding that struggle difficult: the outcome is guaranteed, the grace of God is there, and the day will come when the struggle is over.

Jesus' great high-priestly prayer for us at the Last Supper was a prayer for our unity:

> I pray not only for these,
> but for those also
> who through their words will believe in me.
> May they all be one.
> Father, may they be one in us,
> as you are in me and I am in you,
> so that the world may believe it was you who sent me.
> I have given them the glory you gave to me,
> that they may be one as we are one.
> With me in them and you in me,
> may they be so completely one
> that the world will realize that it was you who sent me
> and that I have loved them as much as you loved me.
> (Jn. 17:20–23)

The whole meaning and direction of our spiritual growth is a movement from isolation and alienation into greater unity with each other. At Holy Communion, each of us receives the body of Christ, and being one with the body of Christ, we shall become one with each other. This is a symbolic prophecy of the mysterious and joyous transformation of our bodies at the Resurrection, when our bodies will become the perfect means of communication and oneness.

In his book on sexual theology, James Nelson tells us:

> Your body which you often reject is accepted by that which
>   is greater than you.
> Your sexual feelings and unfulfilled yearnings are accepted.

You are accepted in your ascetic attempts at self–
    justification or in your hedonistic alienation from the
    true meaning of your sexuality.
You are accepted in those moments of sexual fantasy which
    come unbidden and which delight and disturb you.
You are accepted in your femininity and in your
    masculinity and you have elements of both.
Simply accept the fact that you are accepted as a sexual
    person.
If that happens to you, you experience grace.[4]

Almighty God, our Father and Mother in heaven, thank you for the gift of our body and its sexuality. Through the Resurrection of your son, Jesus, help us to heal our fear of and alienation from our body, help us to trust in the goodness of your creation. Help us to celebrate our sexual existence. Grant us the grace to integrate our sexuality into our drive toward union with you for all eternity in heaven. Amen.

15

Sex as Play

Come then, my love, my lovely one, come. For see, winter is past, the rains are over and gone. The flowers appear on the earth. The season of glad songs has come, and the cooing of the turtledove is heard in our land.

Song of Songs 2:10–12

As James Nelson points out in his book *Between Two Gardens: Reflections on Sexuality and Religious Experience*,[1] the period in which we live today falls between the time of the Garden of Eden depicted in Genesis 2 and the post-Redemption, erotic garden depicted in the Song of Songs. A careful reading of Genesis 2 leaves no doubt that God intended all expressions of human sexuality to be expressions of play. Play and sexual love have always been closely linked. The ancient Sanskrit term for coitus, *kridaratnam*, translates literally as "the jewel of games." Eskimos speak of a sexual encounter as "laughing together." And in certain gay circles back in the fifties, it was common to initiate a sexual encounter by asking, "Would you like to come home and party with me?" In every age, sex has been seen as "God's gift to the poor."

In Genesis, humans, before sin entered their world, are pictured as perfectly at home in their world, and as completely accepting of their bodies and the body's erotic dimension. They had no trouble integrating sex into their loving companionship with each other in the presence of God. But as a result of the sin of pride, humans became ashamed of and alienated from their bodies. They objectified their own and others' bodies as sexual objects subject to lust and contempt. Sexual activity was transformed from a joyful activity to a form of degradation. (It is significant that in every age, our worst insults have been derived from human sexual activities, for example, cocksucker, cunt, prick, jerk.) Our sex lives ceased to be play and became permeated with shame, contempt, insecurity, and anxiety, and thus became more like work than play.

A central part of God's redemptive plan was to restore the integrity and playfulness of human sexuality. The conditions that make play possible discussed in chapter 13 have a special application to human sexuality. In his book *Song of Love: A Biblical Understanding of Sex,*[2] Helmut Gollwitzer makes the point that a redeemed, wholesome, and playful human sexuality is portrayed beautifully in the biblical text of the Song of Songs. Gollwitzer notes that the love extolled in this text is an illicit love. The lovers are not married and are of different races:

"Look," says the Bible, "see these two lovers, how they delight in each other, each pleased with the body of the other. How excited they are as each gazes at the full length of the other's naked body. How they yearn for night to come so that they can embrace and be united. They are Adam and Eve in paradise, free of shame, in the happiness of sex. This is the way it was intended. . . . How could you possibly regard that as sinful? Why would you equate sensuality with immorality? Look at how all their senses are brought into play—seeing, hearing, smelling, tasting, touching! This sensuality is the morality of their love because it is a love as God wants it to be, a fully human love, planned for human beings.

"There is nothing subhuman or animal about it, no relic of the earthly to be painfully endured, as if we have to strive to become purely spiritual beings. Nothing is so unlike the animals as human sexuality. It is not confined to times of being in heat, nor does it merely serve the continuation of the species. It is not limited to the specific genital activity of procreation but encompasses the entire person in an act of complete concentration on and attention to the sex partner."[3]

Gollwitzer points out that even if the Song of Songs extols an illicit kind of love, outside an extrinsically imposed set of rules, it does not give us carte blanche to engage in a totally unstructured and uninhibited sexuality. There is a structure present in the sexuality of the Song of Songs, but it is a structure that is no longer legalistic and repressive, but rather based in the very nature of what it means to be human and compatible with the true freedom of the Gospels. This structure is identical with the conditions for human play I discussed in chapter 13. First of all, play activity must be meaningful in itself and not be related to a result that lies beyond the playful action. Healthy, playful human sex requires that the sex partners treat each other as ends in themselves; a failure to do so reduces one's partner to an object. To deal with any human as a means rather than an end in him- or herself is to degrade and demean that person. The essential immorality of prostitution is not that it involves sex outside of marriage, but that it involves one person using another as an object and the other allowing him- or herself to be used.

This is also the essential flaw in the traditional work-related sexual ethics based on procreation. Any sexual act undertaken exclusively for the purpose of procreation both destroys the play value of sex and reduces the partners to workers interested solely in making a product. It is interesting to note that there is no mention of procreation anywhere in the Song of Songs or in chapter 2 of Genesis.

As we have seen, the conditions necessary for play to exist are identical to the conditions necessary for love to exist between two persons. The most important of these conditions is that the partners see each other as equals. Whenever the man sees himself as superior to the woman, a necessary condition for true love and playfulness within the sexual encounter is absent. In the Song of Songs, the woman's equal status with her lover is striking. It is not an accident that the book begins with the woman's passionate words: "Your lips cover me with kisses; your love is better than wine" (1:2). As Gollwitzer points out, this equality between the partners keeps them from ever pressuring or manipulating each other. Each invites the other to a sexual encounter but profoundly respects the other's freedom: "The other is always wanted as a person, a partner, not as a thing, a means for sexual gratification. No one is reduced to a mere sexual object. All expressions of affection are appeals to the free emotions of the beloved, voicing the hope that the other will respond with the same love."[4]

Recent psychodynamic theory recognizes that the basic human drive is not toward pleasure but toward intimacy. Consequently, the sex drive is the physical dimension of a human need to escape isolation and alienation for a profound physical and spiritual unity. The search for sexual fulfillment is thus one manifestation of a search for unity with God. And achieving that intimacy results in intense pleasure, both physical and spiritual.

I still remember an event that took place almost fifty years ago on my first day in high school. I was a scared, lonely thirteen-year-old, starved for affection, and one day I was placing my books in my locker in the basement when suddenly someone, I never knew who, came around the corner and caught me from behind in a bearhug for a fleeting moment and then disappeared. I shall never forget the profound pleasure I felt in that affectionate and erotic hug. I think I spent the rest of that year putting books in my locker and taking them out again hoping for the return of the mystery hugger, but to no avail.

There is yet another condition that must be met for a sexual encounter to be playful, namely, that one's partner be loved as a unique individual. The bull does not care which cow it mates with; any cow will do. But humans *do* care about the uniqueness of their sexual partner. One's partner is not simply a representative of the opposite sex or the same sex, interchangeable with any other, a mere sex object. Rather, one's partner is a unique and irreplaceable "thou," one particular person whose place no other can take. This man, this woman, this person alone is loved.

This attitude contrasts sharply with the "playboy" view of sex. Those who subscribe to this view feel free to use—and even abuse—their partners selfishly without any sense of responsibility or concern. The perfect playboy cartoon shows a man and woman naked in bed together with the man asking the woman, "Why talk about love at a time like this?" This attitude is perfectly symbolized by the playboy bunny costume, which, with its tail and ears, is an ideal way to dehumanize and depersonalize one's sexual object.

Intimacy, both physical and spiritual, is precisely the goal of playful sex. But as we have seen, in order to have the freedom to play and to overcome self-consciousness, one must have the felt security of being loved. The primary purpose of a relationship of love is to enable the partners to affirm each other continuously through shared activities in an atmosphere of security and trust. Love gives us this freedom.

Those who hold an old-fashioned, dualistic view of love tend to posit a sharp division between spiritual love, which is directed toward the person, and the purely physical gratification of the sex drive. In reality there are not two different kinds of love—all genuine love has its physical aspect. There are, however, two kinds of sex—alpha sex and omega sex—that need to be distinguished. Alpha sex involves using one's partner selfishly to obtain one's own sexual satisfaction. This kind of sexual activity never results in true intimacy and provides no escape from loneliness; on the contrary, it intensifies loneliness. Clients have told me many times that their sense of isolation only increased after an all-night orgy in a gay bath house.

Omega sex, on the other hand, occurs when there is a complete fusion of sensual and personal love. Each partner is a source of pleasure for the other and each can experience pleasure only by being a source of pleasure for the other. As Gollwitzer puts it: "Self-centeredness—I need that person for myself, for my own happiness—is the *power* of eros, whereas the knowledge that I will be happy only through the happiness of my partner is the *wisdom* of eros. Eros understands that we get what we want, not simply when or if the partner's wants are also met, but precisely in and through their being met."[5]

As a psychotherapist, I am intensely aware that I am dealing here with an ideal goal of human sexual growth and maturity. As Nelson notes, most of us find ourselves at some place between the two gardens, aspiring to omega sex but practicing alpha sex, but hopefully growing daily in our ability to integrate our sexual activity into our capacity for love.

I am also aware that many people are psychically so injured that they are incapable of a full human relationship of intimacy and love. Yet these persons have a right to some playful expression of their sexuality. I agree with Norman Pittenger that there are only three kinds of sexual activity between consenting adults: good, better, and best sex. Apart from rape or child abuse, it is difficult to sin seriously in a sexual gesture. I am reminded of a joke I heard years ago about a derelict who went into a bar on the Bowery and said to all the drinkers at the bar: "I'll go to bed with anyone who guesses the weight of my parakeet!" One man lifted his head from the bar and said: "Two hundred pounds." "Close enough!" the derelict answered. The humor of the joke is that it speaks to every one of us in our loneliness. Two lonely people, both too wounded at that point in their life to form an intimate relationship, will know a moment of affection and a sharing of sexual pleasure, and that is good.

Gay Sexual Liberation

Like the love of the man and woman in the Song of Songs, all gay sexual love has been illicit, condemned by the laws of society and the church. Because of this, gay and lesbian sexual love has had no models or rules to go by. With the Stonewall revolution, the gay and lesbian community undertook an all-out celebration of gay sexuality and a constant exploration of new forms of sexual fulfillment. Since any and all forms of gay sex were considered by heterosexist society to be illegal and immoral by their very nature, the gay community was not prepared to recognize any moral or legal restraints on its sexual behavior.

At its best, the gay sexual revolution freed sexual expression from all artificial restraints and restored it to its proper human context of joyous play. And since gay sex takes place between two members of the same sex, many found no difficulty in seeing their sex partner as their equal. There was a constant effort to overcome those restraints on sexual behavior that were proper to a heterosexual context and did not belong in a gay or lesbian context. For example, many asked whether monogamy was the best model for gay couples. Does the concept that there should be no sex outside the relationship have to do only with the need of establishing the paternity of a child? Many gay couples I have counseled discovered that, at least early on in a relationship, monogamy and fidelity played a necessary role in building the kind of trust that made the vulnerability of true human love possible. But some found that once that trust was established, an open relationship enhanced rather than threatened the relationship.

I still feel, as I stated in *The Church and the Homosexual,* that a committed, faithful, loving relationship as the ideal context for all human sexual expression is based in the nature of being human.[6] "It is not good that the man should be alone. I will make him a helpmate" (Gn. 2:18). I do not see this as imposing a heterosexual norm on gay people. I believe that we are dealing with a fundamental need built into human nature that has to do with the development of trust and love and the greatest possible development of psychic maturity and health. Sexual activity can only reach its perfection as loving, joyous play within such a context. However, I am aware of many gay and lesbian people who are incapable for many different reasons—psychological, social, or economic—of entering into such a committed relationship. The best many of these people are capable of is a "one night stand" or an occasional sexual liaison with a friend.

Sexual Liberation and the AIDS Crisis

The first reaction of the gay community to AIDS has been a serious reevaluation of its efforts toward sexual liberation. There is a welcome and necessary new emphasis on prudence and health consciousness in all sexual expression. There is also a new exploration of the kind of committed relationship that is appropriate to lesbian women and gay men and is not just a repetition of heterosexual models. The majority of gay and lesbian people today are consciously seeking for a lover. The danger in the present situation is that many in the gay community could lose the freshness and the joy of their celebration of God's good gift of sexuality and regress into feelings of shame, guilt, and loathing for any expression of their sexuality. The possibility of having caring, playful sex still exists if both partners carefully follow the guidelines for safer sex.

As I mentioned in *The Church and the Homosexual,* a paradoxical result of the AIDS crisis is that it is bringing gay love out of the closet.[7] Before AIDS, the most visible members of the gay and lesbian community were those who frequented the gay discos, bars, and baths. These were the people associated with the so-called gay life-style. Those who were involved in loving, committed relationships for the most part remained closeted in order to protect each other's jobs, homes, and family from the consequences of public exposure.

AIDS has forced many couples to be public about their relationships. I personally know many priests, ministers, hospital personnel, and family members who have been astonished at the depth of the love, mutual support, and self-sacrifice that characterizes the relationship of most gay couples.

Every element of the moral, sexual love-making portrayed in the Song of Songs can be, and frequently is, present in the sexual relationship of two gay men or two lesbian women who love each other. Consequently, there is no reason why their sexual unions should not be as accepted, respected, and valued by the church and by society. Near the end of the Song of Songs we read:

> Set me like a seal on your heart,
> like a seal on your arm.
> For love is strong as Death,
> jealously relentless as Sheol.
> The flash of it is a flash of fire,
> a flame of Yahweh himself.
> Love no flood can quench,
> no torrents drown.
> Were a man to offer all the wealth of his house to buy love,
> contempt is all he would purchase. (8:6–7)

A loving, playful sexual encounter can become the locus of a mystical experience of the divine. We will all have learned an important lesson when we realize that the essential quality of such an encounter is the love involved, not the gender of the partners. In other words, it's the person that counts, not the plumbing.

Almighty God, restore in us our unity with our sexual body so that once again we may experience the joyful and holy play of sex in your presence. Amen.

16

The Relationship between Mary, the Mother of God, and the Gay and Lesbian Community

I've always had a strong intuition that there is a special relationship between Mary and those of us who are lesbian and gay, if for no other reason because, in the Magnificat, Mary identifies herself with the *anowim*, the exiles, the outcasts, the poor and the powerless:

> His mercy reaches from age to age for those who fear him.
> He has shown the power of his arm,
> he has routed the proud of heart.
> He has pulled down the princes from their throne and
>   exalted the lowly.
> The hungry he has filled with good things, the rich sent
>   empty away.
> (Lk. 1:50–53)

Recently, during prayer and meditation, other aspects of that affinity of gays to Mary have become clear to me. It is interesting to note that psychotherapists have pointed out the special family pattern that frequently accompanies gayness. That pattern is one of the close-binding mother and the distant, emotionally uninvolved father. Although this pattern frequently accompanies gayness, the claim by some conservative psychiatrists that it is the *cause* of homosexuality has been thoroughly discredited. I am more inclined to believe that this pattern is not the cause of gayness but a result.

For example, because the young boy is gay and in touch with the feminine or *anima* dimension of himself, his father becomes remote, uninterested, and unavailable. In fact, the father often actively avoids a gay son whose effeminacy he finds repulsive. This is the same male figure to whom the gay son, in a reverse of the normal oedipal attraction, feels a strong attachment. This attachment can later become foundation for a masochistic attraction to the straight male who is rejecting in adult life. In contrast, the mother appreciates the sensitive nature of her gay son, finds him a good companion, and draws close emotionally and protectively to him.

It is understandable that the gay man who has had such an experience with his parents would find it psychologically easy to approach the blessed mother in prayer and feel assured of a kind and loving reception. Mary has always symbolized the maternal side of God—loving, kind, merciful, nonjudgmental, compassionate, healing, and easily approachable.

I am aware that Mary is a spiritual resource primarily for those brought up in the Catholic or Orthodox religious traditions. Most gays and lesbians brought up in the Protestant tradition are not familiar with devotion to the mother of God. This was the result of a legitimate reaction against theological excesses in the claims made for Mary's power. For example, some Catholics claimed for her the title of co-redemptrix, which would have implied a more than human status for Mary and an equal role with her son Jesus in our salvation.

Protestants rightfully proclaimed that there is only one redeemer of the human race, only one person who shared both human and divine nature, namely, Jesus. But I am inclined to think that in their fervor to protect the unique status of Jesus, Protestants have on occasion been guilty of throwing the baby out with the bathwater. All Christian communities are now aware that there was an overemphasis in the past on the paternal nature of God, and are involved in a major struggle to reclaim the feminine dimension of God. Allowing Mary to play a role in our spiritual lives will help restore the balance.

There is another aspect to devotion to Mary, however, from which I would like to distance myself, an aspect that has been very destructive to the psychic health and well-being of women and, consequently, of all of us. This is the image of Mary as totally passive, docile, and asexual. This model, which has frequently been held up as something for women to emulate, has been used to deny women the right to sexual fulfillment, an equal role with men, and the right to full self-realization.

I prefer the Mary of the Magnificat—that Mary has a passion for justice and a feisty spirit. The Mary who yearns to see princes pulled down from their thrones, the proud routed, and the rich sent away empty while the poor are filled with good things is more likely to be involved today in issues of social justice and the movement for human liberation. I always use the Magnificat as a litmus test for the validity of any message purporting to come from Mary, and I find suspect any modern message that has none of the Magnificat's passion for justice and concern for the poor and powerless.

The document "Partners in the Mystery of Redemption: A Pastoral Response to Women's Concerns for Church and Society," issued in April 1988 by the National Conference of Catholic Bishops, is a sign of real hope for all those interested in lesbian and gay liberation. There is a very strong link between the liberation of women and gay liberation; in fact, one cannot succeed without the other. When we hear the bishops indict the church for centuries of sinful institutional and structural sexism, there is hope that the recognition of centuries of institutional and structural homophobia is not far behind.

All my life I have found a unique spiritual resource in Mary, as intercessor before Jesus and through him before the throne of God. That special role has a strong biblical foundation, which can be found in the account of Jesus' miracle of changing water into wine at the marriage feast of Cana (Jn. 2:1–12).

In that account, Jesus came with his disciples to help a young couple celebrate their nuptial feast, which in Jewish tradition could last three days. Jesus' mother Mary was also among the guests. She was the first to observe the embarrassment of the young couple when they ran out of wine to serve their guests.

Mary immediately went to her son and said simply, "They have no wine." Jesus seemed almost annoyed with his mother and the implicit request that he do something to relieve the embarrassment of the young couple: "Woman, why turn to me? My hour has not come yet." The implication is clearly that the miracle would not have taken place if it had not been for Mary's sensitivity and her ability to persuade her son to use his power. We are then told that Jesus told the servants to fill six stone jars, each of which could hold twenty to thirty gallons of water, a total of 120 to 180 gallons of water. At Jesus' command the water blushed to wine, enough to fill a wine shop, and wine of such quality that the steward chastised the bridegroom for saving the best wine for last. The moral of the story in Christian tradition has been, If you want something done that seems to be almost impossible to accomplish, get Mary on your side, have her plead for you with her son, Jesus, and you will get what you want.

Psychologists point out that the roots of our psychic, often unconscious, image of God the father are to be found in our experience of our human father. We unconsciously project onto God the same attitudes and feelings that we experienced from our father. Beavers[1] points out that children who have had good, loving parenting can "defang the poison of religion" and learn to receive only its good and loving message. However, those children who have had inadequate parenting are exposed to the harsher side of religion and can very easily end up with a frightening, guilt-inducing image of God the father. These same psychologists point out that we form another ego image of God as a God of love, and frequently the root of that image is found in our experience of our mother's love. In the Catholic tradition, this maternal side of God can be split off from the image of God the father and projected unto Mary, our mother in heaven. This feeling is reflected in one of my favorite prayers, the Memorare:

Remember, O most gracious Virgin Mary
that never was it known
that anyone who fled to thy protection,
implored thy help, or sought thy intercession
was left unaided.
Inspired by this confidence,
I fly unto thee, O Virgin of virgins, my mother,
before thee I come, sinful and sorrowful.

O Mother of the Word incarnate
despise not my petitions,
but in your mercy hear and answer me. Amen.

My feelings toward God the father and Mary our mother
were compounded when I grew up and I became aware that I
was gay and that the church condemned that orientation as evil.
For those in a similar situation, fear of God the father's rejection
frequently becomes very intense, blocking off one's ability to
enter into God's presence in prayer. Throughout that experience,
Mary remained my refuge and my strength.

The most popular prayer to Mary among Catholics is the
Hail Mary, a very simple prayer that begins with Gabriel's words
at the Annunciation and ends with a petition for Mary's prayers
for us:

Hail Mary full of grace.
The lord is with you.
Blessed are you among women,
and blessed is the fruit of your womb, Jesus.

Holy Mary, Mother of God,
pray for us sinners,
now and at the hour of our death. Amen.

I sometimes wonder if there is not a deep unconscious reason
why gay men in touch with the feminine dimension of themselves sometimes refer to each other as "Mary." I know that that
term is most often used as a put-down, a term of contempt, but
perhaps beneath the surface there lies an awareness of a special
relationship to the mother of God. In any case, I recommend that
that term take on a positive and affirming meaning.

My own childhood experience of my mother's death when I
was three years old gave my devotion to Mary, my mother in
heaven, a special emphasis. After she died, I was told that my
mother, whose name was also Mary, was now in heaven where
she would pray for me and protect me. As a result I tended to
combine my human mother, Mary, with Mary the mother of
God in my thoughts, feelings, and prayers.

Even when my fear of God and my feelings of guilt about
my sexuality became most intense and tended to cut me off from
God the father, I always felt close to Mary, my mother. On at
least one occasion, that feeling of closeness saved my sanity. As a

prisoner of war, I was sent with a group of prisoners into Berlin during the Allied bombing raids to help dig out bodies from the rubble and bury them. Our guards, resentful of the Allied air superiority, would not allow us American prisoners to spend the night in a bomb shelter but made us sleep unprotected on the surface during the raids, which occurred nearly every night. Luckily, the Christian brothers who were my high school teachers at Saint Joseph's Collegiate Institute had demanded that we commit the poetry we were studying to memory, and I had memorized a long segment of Coleridge's "Rime of the Ancient Mariner." Despite the anti-aircraft guns blazing, the searchlights zigzagging across the sky, the hundreds of aircraft engines roaring above and the explosion of bombs, I was able to go to sleep peacefully each night by reciting these words:

> Oh sleep! It is a gentle thing,
> Beloved from pole to pole!
> To Mary Queen the praise be given!
> She sent the gentle sleep from Heaven,
> That slid into my soul.

The Beloved Disciple

There is another figure with whom the gay community has a special relationship, similar to its relationship to Mary, and that figure is John, the one person among Jesus' disciples with whom we as gay people can frequently identify. If he was not actually gay himself, he is certainly depicted as having had a gay sensitivity. He always refers to himself as "the disciple whom Jesus loved." Note that John does not say that he had a special love for Jesus; rather, he states that there was a special kind of love that Jesus had for him that differed from the love that Jesus obviously had for the other eleven disciples.

John records the fact that at the Last Supper, when Jesus announced that one of them was about to betray him, John reclined next to Jesus and leaned on his breast: "The disciple Jesus loved was reclining next to Jesus; Simon Peter signed to him and said, 'Ask who it is he means,' so leaning back on Jesus' breast he said, 'Who is it, Lord?'" (Jn. 13:23–25). Obviously Peter recognized the special relationship between Jesus and John. Another indication of this relationship is the fact that John ran ahead of

Peter and was the first after the women to see the empty tomb and know that Jesus had risen. On still another occasion, while fishing with Peter in Galilee after the Resurrection, John was the first to recognize Jesus when he appeared on the shore (Jn. 21:7).

John alone of all the male disciples stood under the cross and tried to comfort Jesus. And it was to John that Jesus entrusted the care of his mother after his death: "Seeing his mother and the disciple he loved standing near her, Jesus said to his mother, 'Woman, this is your son.' Then to the disciple he said, 'This is your mother.' And from that moment, the disciple made a place for her in his home" (Jn. 19:26–27). And we are told that John took Mary into his home and cared for her until her assumption into heaven. Over the centuries, how many lesbian women and gay men have been the ones who stayed at home and took care of their aging parents? Every family that has a gay son or a lesbian daughter is indeed blessed.

Finally, we must not forget that Mary herself was a member of the sexually disenfranchised. First of all, she was sexually unique, the only virgin mother in history. Then, to all appearances she was an unwed mother and thus liable to the severe penalties of Jewish law. Mary, from her personal experience, can understand the fears and the pain of our gay exiled status.

Holy Mary, Queen of Heaven, pray for all us queens here on earth—and all us queers, fags, dykes, fems, fairies, fruits, transvestites, transsexuals, and all sexual exiles. For in many ways we are your special children.

Part Six

Unto Dust You
Shall Return

Introduction: AIDS and the
Acceptance of Human Mortality

Since all the children share the same blood and flesh, [Jesus] too shared equally in it, so that by his death he could . . . set free all those who had been held in slavery all their lives by the fear of death.

Hebrews 2:14–15

AIDS has forced us all to face our mortality. As much as we might want to deny this fact, we can no longer do so. As John Snow observes in his book *Mortal Fear: Meditations on Death and AIDS:* "Unlike nuclear war, it is not a vague threat out there in the maze of high technology. It is among us, killing some of us, and some of our friends, leaving us randomly vulnerable to our environment, making us terribly manifestly mortal."[1]

The person who continually denies death is in reality completely dominated by the fear of death and is moreover spiritually blind to his or her need for God. AIDS challenges us to acknowledge and accept our mortality. We must face the fear of death; we must stop trying to deny or avoid that fear. The New Testament's most powerful metaphor for sin is being in thrall to the fear of death. Those obsessed with a fear of death will do anything to stay alive; they will obey anyone or swallow any idea that promises them survival.

After I had appeared on a segment of "The Phil Donohue Show" devoted to homosexuality, I said to an antigay fanatic: "You are full of hate!" He answered: "I'd rather be full of hate than dead!" I responded: "I have news for you. You're dead already!" As Snow remarks, all fear has its ultimate origin in the fear of death. "The ego, the conscious, willing center of our being, will make self-defence its primary concern until it becomes reconciled to its mortality."[2]

If we are able to deal with this mortal fear, we will recover our humanity as well. The AIDS crisis has reminded us of an ancient lesson that most modern, industrialized societies have forgotten. Every healthy culture continually mitigates the fear of death through its customs and rituals. These practices, such as the Ash Wednesday rite of placing ashes on the forehead, remind us that death is an integral part of the human condition and help us to control our fears and accept our mortal destiny.

Our alienation from our body and its sexuality is at root an alienation from the mortality of our body. To overcome that alienation and to be able to accept our body in all its dimensions, including the sexual, we must become reconciled with our humanity in its wholeness, including death.

The following three chapters are reflections on various aspects of death, the purpose of which is to help us deal with our fear of death and, when the time comes, to be able to accept death. Chapter 17, "The Christian Understanding of Death, Resurrection, and Time," deals with the complex and paradoxical nature of our relationship to death, which is at once a completely natural part of our human history and yet something we cannot accept as our ultimate destiny. Chapter 18, "Reflections on Judgment," deals with an important aspect of our pathological fear of death, namely, a distorted understanding of God's role as judge that results in an inordinate fear of death. Chapter 19, "Reflections on Mourning," deals with the process of mourning the death of a lover or friend and tries to distinguish the healthy, normal grieving process from its pathological counterpart.

My purpose in these chapters is to reflect on the spiritual resources that we can draw upon to deal with and overcome our fear of death. But I am not counseling passivity in the face of the AIDS crisis. The primary message in these chapters is that overcoming our fear of death enables us to celebrate life. All the psychic energies locked up in denial and repression can be released for a positive commitment to life.

These chapters are also intended to celebrate the courage and action of all those persons with AIDS who are fighting to stay alive and healthy and to enhance the quality of life for themselves and their fellow persons with AIDS.

I have mentioned elsewhere that Jesus' primary commitment was to relieving human suffering and that every follower of Jesus should be committed to the same goal. Consequently, we would be remiss in our Christian duty if we did not do everything in our power to *stop* the epidemic, to find a cure, and in the meantime to search out every means possible to prolong life, relieve suffering, and put up a good fight.

17

The Christian Understanding of Death, Resurrection, and Time

> *For I am certain of this: neither death nor life, no angel, no prince, nothing that exists, nothing still to come, not any power, or height or depth, nor any created thing, can ever come between us and the love of God made visible in Christ Jesus our Lord.*
>
> Romans 8:38–39

The season of Lent has a mystical quality about it; it is a time when we seem to come very close to God. We begin Lent with a stark reminder of death and our mortality: "Remember human, that you are dust and unto dust you shall return." During this holy season, we are all invited to reflect deeply on the ultimate meaning of our life and our death. Lent recalls the forty days

Jesus spent in the desert fasting and fighting off the temptations of greed, attachment, power, pride, and pleasure. He had to distinguish what was important from what was not and, finally, he had to confront his destiny.

During Lent the churches put a special emphasis on the need we have of God's help to undertake any process of spiritual growth or change. The Lenten prayer from the ancient Syriac liturgy speaks of an "original darkness [connected with our sinful condition] that shadows our vision," a native tendency on our part to be blind to true values, to get our priorities all wrong, to fall into the traps Jesus dealt with in the desert. Consequently, we cry out to God: "restore our sight that we may look upon your son, who calls us to redemption and to a change of heart."

Lent is a time for setting priorities, a time to put first things first. It is a time for us to recall that the ultimate meaning of our life and death is to bring us into the intimate presence of God. Most of us spend much of our lives avoiding death and pretending we are immortal. The very thought of death provokes such fear and anxiety in us that we instinctively repress the thought. As Ernest Becker points out in his book *The Denial of Death*,[1] a certain degree of denial is healthy and normal, especially in the young.

But a part of spiritual growth and maturity consists of confronting our fear of death, bringing that fear into full consciousness, and trying with God's grace to lessen its control over our lives. We are called on to stop ignoring and hiding from that ultimate meaning; to accept our destiny of death and rebirth and to reaffirm our faith: Christ has robbed death of its power and brought us eternal life.

Edward Schillebeeckx tells us in his book *Christ: The Experience of Jesus as Lord*[2] that death, as the conclusion of a human life, ought to signify integration, unity, and wholeness. Most of the time, however, we do not see death this way. Rather, we see it as the disappearance and annihilation of the individual. We humans seem to be the only creatures who have a conscious awareness of our death, and that awareness gives an emotional significance to every moment of our lives.

There is an instinctive human protest against the absurdity and scandal of death, a fact that is reflected in the ancient Christian belief that death entered our world through the sin of Adam and Eve. The reign of death in this world represents in some mysterious way the reign of Satan. We refuse to understand ourselves as a fleeting personally insignificant and replaceable element in history.

However, the fact that Jesus himself became reconciled to his mortality, that he accepted his destiny of death on a cross, and that in and through his death he became reconciled with God, makes it clear to us that within the boundaries of human history redemption can never be achieved by trying to escape from our mortality. From a human point of view, redemption essentially implies reconciliation with one's own mortality coupled with radical love. Human love has somehow been endowed by Jesus with the power to overcome death. Our belief in resurrection does not deny that even for Christians death is still an impenetrable mystery and suffering. Jesus himself experienced that suffering and voiced the instinctive human protest against death in the agony in the garden.

I believe it was Woody Allen who once remarked that an atheist differs from a believer because an atheist has "no invisible means of support." What *is* our invisible means of support? Religious belief in certain victory over death has always been based in a living, experiential communion of life between God and humanity. Those who have not had this experiential communion will tend to reject the possibility of resurrection as ungrounded or meaningless, or else as mere wish-fulfillment, because nonreligious human experience cannot offer any evidence for this belief. We Christians see the hope of resurrection as a gracious offer of saving communion by God—an offer that we are free to accept or reject. The essential point is that even death cannot destroy a true, living communion with the living God. The kingdom of the dead does not have the last word in our personal history. Life with God is stronger than death.

Victory over death should never be understood as a human claim, but as a special gift of God. Our hope of overcoming death is not justified by any merit on our part, but is based rather on the goodness of the living God revealed to us in the death and resurrection of Jesus. We can find support for our faith in life after death in the revealed word of God and in our personal experience of love, both human and divine. Our faith and hope are grounded in the nature and the activity of God. Jesus' resurrection thus becomes for us a sure sign of God's power over death and love for us.

Death and the Meaning of Time

I would like next to address the question of whether there is a felt need in our lives to which God's promise of resurrection and bodily immortality is a vital response.

Some people try to view human life and death objectively, as natural events in the cycle of growth and decay. They urge us to accept our own death as part of the natural order of things. On the other hand, some scientists believe that they may soon be able to extend human life indefinitely. Professor Esfandiary of the New School in an op-ed article in the *New York Times* entitled "Sorry, We're Here for Eternity!" writes: "Why exhort people to accept finitude at the very moment in evolution when at long last we can triumph over our supreme tragedy? We who in the 20th century . . . can now marshal our genius to achieve the most transcendent and liberating freedom, physical immortality." Esfandiary believes that by control of the aging process, replacement of worn-out body parts, and joining humans to machines, human life can be prolonged indefinitely. We are rapidly approaching a time when we may have to choose to die—something that has been prefigured in recent "right-to-die" cases. The disturbing assumption here is that humanity's desire for immortality can somehow be fulfilled by indefinitely extending our physical existence in time.

Because we deny death so vigorously, we may begin to believe in a kind of pseudo-immortality and cease to take death seriously. As Karl Rahner, the Jesuit theologian, observes, "Time becomes madness if it cannot reach fulfillment. To be able to go on forever would be a hell of empty meaninglessness. No moment would have any importance because one could postpone and put everything off until an empty later which would always be there." It is the reality of death that gives every moment of our lives a meaning and urgency that are essential to the quality of human life. The prospect of an unending future also throws a new light on the meaning of the Christian belief in resurrection. For resurrection does not signify merely life without end, but a transformation of time and of our being.

We humans are in thrall to the tyranny of fleeting time; we experience time as a prison from which we long to escape. The past never really exists in the present. Insofar as we are held captive by the past because of guilt and remorse, we are cut off from the present moment. Similarly, insofar as anxiety, insecurity, and fear cause us to brood continually about the future, we are once again cut off from the present.

Our fear of death, then, should be understood not primarily as a need for an indefinite future but as a need to live fully in the present moment, a need whose hope lies in the future. To condemn a human to an indefinite future of fleeting time, the very nature of which would negate the possibility of a real being-there in the present moment, would be to condemn that person to a living hell.

As Nietzsche so well observed, Western culture's loss of faith in the belief that the historical process of time has a revealed meaning and that there is a transcendental significance to the rectilinear progress of the world has rendered time barren, transforming it into a low-grade infinity of succession without beginning or end. When we find ourselves caught up by this empty time, life itself becomes absurd and valueless.

The essential paradox in the human urge to transform time is beautifully expressed in two myths. The first is Plato's myth of the cave. In the *Republic,* Plato pictures humanity as trapped in a cave that represents the world of time, change, and material objects. It is only when we escape from this cave through death that we escape time and enter into the realm of eternal, unchanging ideas and finally experience fulfillment. This concept led to the theory that we are immortal souls destined to receive a beatifying vision of eternal ideas. But Plato's eternity is static and dead, and ignores the reality of our flesh-and-blood existence.

The other story is the Russian folktale, "The Great Stone Flower." In this story, a sculptor spends his life trying to capture the fleeting beauty of a rose in stone. He fails again and again. Finally, a spirit from the netherworld appears to him and leads him down into a cave where he finds a perfect stone flower carved from precious gems. He is so captivated by his vision that he is held in a trance in the unchanging, lifeless world of stone. However, in the world above there is a woman who loves him, and through the power of her love she manages to find the cave, break the sculptor's trance, and lead him back to the surface where love and beauty, although fragile and fleeting, are nonetheless real.

It is marvelous how the concept of resurrection responds to the longings expressed in these two stories. The risen Jesus is, indeed, real; he invites his disciples to touch him, and sits and eats with them to convince them that he is not a ghost. Yet the risen Jesus has also overcome death. He has both transcended time and can enter time at will.

The great mystics have always been aware that time has an extratemporal or supratemporal dimension, the eternal that neither endures nor passes, the *nunc stans,* the paradoxical unity of always and now without past or future. To gain a vision of it or to experience it in some way has always been the supreme mandate of the mystical experience and its interpretation of death. The person whose life has received the seal of this moment of mystical experience has conquered both time and death. Yet this experience is not reserved for exceptional people and extraordinary circumstances. On the contrary, there is a taste of this conquest of death and time in every experience of intense personal love. "I bless you, Father, Lord of heaven and of earth, for hiding these things from the learned and the clever and revealing them to mere children" (Mt. 11:25).

The Contrast between Stoic and Christian Belief

There is a fundamental and necessary connection between human love and the desire for immortality. When two people give and receive genuine love, the happiness they find in this communion is expressed in a spontaneous longing for immortality. Every love poem ever written carries the message, "I am eternally yours!"

The late John Courtney Murray, S.J., once commented that there are only two fundamental responses to life that make sense: the Stoic and the Christian. The basic aim of the Stoic practice of the virtue of indifference was precisely an attempt to overcome the fear of death. In order to be able to welcome death, one had to become detached from life and all the affections that bind one to life. Marcus Aurelius, the Stoic Roman emperor, once sent this message of despair to his subjects: "Remember man that in a little while you will be nobody, nowhere . . . take great consolation in that fact." The greatest threat to this grim tranquility was human love. Thus the fundamental message of Stoic asceticism was "never fall in love," because the lover necessarily desires immortality for him- or herself as well as for the loved one. Musonius Rufus, a Stoic philosopher, even urged husbands not to love their wives lest they lose their tranquil indifference to life.

How great a price, then, must we pay to escape the fear of death? Is it true, as the Stoics among us claim, that we can only escape from that fear by rejecting love itself? Or to put it another way, to what extent do we need to have a sense of hope in the future in order to make a whole-hearted commitment in the present to life and love?

The answer of our Christian faith to these questions is an affirmation of God's promise of resurrection as fulfilled in Jesus Christ. Our faith also makes it quite clear that what we hope in is, from a purely human point of view, absurd, irrational, impossible, unbelievable; that is to say, miraculous.

At the same time, Christians understand that by affirming the resurrection of the flesh, we are also affirming a vital response to a felt human need and a necessary belief. Without this belief we would not have the ability to affirm life or have sufficient hope in the future to sustain the commitment of true, personal love.

The question of whether Christian belief in resurrection and immortality opens up a real future for humanity will have to be proven over and over again. We can give witness to the effectiveness of that belief whenever we make a courageous commitment in imitation of Jesus to do away with suffering wherever we can, to promote justice fearlessly, to heal wounds, and to help liberate all, especially our gay brothers and lesbian sisters, to the fullness of life. The ultimate measure of the depth of our faith is our freedom to give and receive love. The pagan Stoics of the first century after Jesus marveled at the freedom to love present in the early Christian community: "Look, how they love one another!"

AIDS and Mortality

Psychologists are aware that one of the deepest roots of homophobia in the unconscious has to do with the fear of death. The primary instinctive escape from death is through procreation: one achieves immortality through one's progeny. Consequently, lesbians and gay men, since they usually do not procreate, can unconsciously represent mortality.

In the Old Testament God's original covenant with his chosen people was a procreative covenant. They were to "be fruitful, multiply" until their descendants were as numerous as the grains of sand by the sea (Gn. 1:28). From among those descendants would eventually come the Messiah. As a result of this belief, eunuchs and all those who did not marry and bear children were excluded from membership in the community (Deuteronomy). The greatest blessing God could bestow was fertility, and the greatest curse was barrenness. But once the Messiah arrived, he would establish a new covenant between God and humanity based in the hope of immortality through resurrection.

Thus Isaiah predicts that, after the Messiah comes, eunuchs will be accepted as full members in the new community: "I will give [them], in my house and within my walls . . . an everlasting name that shall never be effaced" (56:4–6). In chapter 19, verse 12 of Matthew Jesus makes it clear that the term *eunuch* applies to all those who are sexually different and who, for whatever reason, do not procreate: "There are eunuchs born that way from their mother's womb, there are eunuchs made so by men and there are eunuchs who have made themselves that way for the sake of the kingdom of heaven." Isaiah's prophecy comes true when in Acts 8:26 the Holy Spirit leads Phillip out to baptize the eunuch who is reading Isaiah, the prophet who had foretold that all those who are sexually different will have a special place in the house of the Lord.

I see today's lesbian and gay Christian movement as the literal fulfillment of that prophecy. Scripture itself links the nonprocreative status of lesbians and gays to the hope of resurrection.

As we have seen, Genesis portrays Adam and Eve becoming alienated from their bodies and ashamed of their sexuality because of the fear of death. Gay people have always held to half the truth about our human body: we have tended to accept the sanity of living out an embodied existence as fully as we can. We have identified with the body, and especially with its sexual dimension.

Now the AIDS epidemic has once again linked homosexuality with mortality, and gay people are being called on to give a special witness to the meaning of death and the hope of resurrection. John Fortunato, in his book *AIDS: The Spiritual Dilemma,* sees one benefit for humanity arising from the scourge of AIDS, namely, to teach us once again the truth of mortality: "If this nightmare brings back to our consciousness the resurrection hope without which life is so much courageous despair, then in the groaning of creation, with tears and sighs, perhaps the Holy

Spirit will usher in some modicum of peace or even a corner of salvation that might otherwise have been unobtainable."[3]

Because the normal escapes from mortality—disembodiment and procreation—have been closed off for them, lesbians and gays are left with only one choice: to despair or to trust in God's power and promise and become a resurrection people. In the midst of the crisis, persons with AIDS are bearing witness to the preciousness of life and showing true courage in the face of death. In my own pastoral experience I am aware of the special spiritual peace, joy, and trust with which so many persons with AIDS have faced death. It is this spiritual confidence that has allowed many to give themselves over to celebrating life and enhancing its quality for themselves and others.

We have yet another source of hope and comfort in the promise of the Resurrection, which frees us to love, and in our experience of love we touch immortality because we touch the living reality of God.

> My dear people,
> let us love one another
> since love comes from God
> and everyone who loves is begotten by God and knows
>   God.
> Anyone who fails to love can never have known God,
> because God is love.
> God's love for us was revealed
> when God sent into the world his only Son
> so that we could have life through him;
> this is the love I mean:
> not our love for God,
> but God's love for us when he sent his Son
> to be the sacrifice that takes our sins away.
> My dear people,
> since God has loved us so much,
> we too should love one another.
> No one has ever seen God;
> But as long as we love one another
> God will live in us
> and his love will be complete in us.
> We can know that we are living in him

and he is living in us
because he lets us share his Spirit.
   (1 Jn. 4:7–13)

Teihard de Chardin, the Jesuit paleontologist and theologian, writes in his book *Hymn of the Universe:*

> Death will not simply throw us back into the great flux of reality as the pantheist picture of beatitude would have us believe. Nevertheless in death we are caught up, overwhelmed, dominated by the divine power which lies within the forces of inner integration and, above all, within the irresistible yearning which will drive the human spirit on to complete its further predestined journey as infallibly as the sun causes the mist to rise from the water on which it shines.
> Death surrenders us completely to God. It makes us pass into God. In return we have to surrender ourselves to it, in love and in the abandon of love; since, when death comes to us, there is nothing further for us to do but let ourselves be entirely dominated and led onward by God.[4]

I would like once again to end on a personal note. One of the people I love most deeply is my sister, Sister Sheila, who is two years older than I. Sis took care of me when I was a child, and from the time she entered the convent over forty-five years ago, she has prayed for me and enlisted the prayers of her community and the various charismatic prayer groups to which she belongs on behalf of my ministry to my lesbian sisters and gay brothers. I have been extremely grateful for all that prayer, which I know has been extremely effective.

My sister has undergone an incredible amount of physical suffering because of a bone condition that threatens to immobilize her. She has had innumerable operations that have had frequent complications. She once shared with me a passage that meant a great deal to her:

> Once we know that suffering has a purpose, or at least we can believe that there is a meaning to it, we can endure much worse. That is the Gospel message—that suffering need not be a loss. People can grow better through suffering, and can also become beautiful, and the latter serves as a grace

to others. Their suffering has made them transparent, more open, wise and gentle. In them, we see the fruitfulness of the cross. Pain can glorify us, make us radiant and give a fruitfulness to our lives.

Pain has certainly given my sister an enviable spiritual power and freedom. Recently she told me of the following episode, which occurred while she was on her annual retreat. On the first day of the retreat, she found herself in a profound depression that felt like death itself. This depression lasted all day, and no matter how she tried she could not lift it. Exhausted after a day spent in depressed suffering, she returned to her room and began to write in her diary the events, thoughts, and feelings of that day. Suddenly she began to write rapidly, and she felt that someone else was using her hand to write. These were the words she read after the automatic writing ended:

> Sheila, don't be afraid of death. I have freed you of many things, so that you can prayerfully prepare for my kingdom. Have no fear because your goodness and love for me have far outweighed your faults and mistakes.
>
> Continue to love me with your great love and the generosity of your life that you have given to me. You are beautiful to me. I love you with a deep love because you have accepted my will. I will continue to love and bless you. Do not be afraid. I will be with you always to give you the courage and the strength you need.

My sister told me that, from that moment, the depression lifted and she has since known a wonderful joy and lightness of heart and feels ready for anything that might come along.

Almighty God, free us all from the fear of death. Grant us your gifts of peace, trust, and courage. Help us to affirm life joyously in the face of death with the confidence that your love will overcome death and lead us into eternal life. Amen.

18

Reflections on Judgment

I shall indeed be with you soon. Amen; come, Lord Jesus.
Revelation 22:20

During the Christmas season, the Christian community looks in two directions. It looks back to the first coming of Christ, our savior, in his birth as the infant Jesus in Bethlehem. And it looks forward to the Second Coming, when Jesus will come again in power and glory to carry out his task as judge. That will be the ultimate epiphany, or showing forth, of Jesus' divine power, foreshadowed in the feast of the three kings.

I would like to reflect with you on the meaning of that second coming for each of us, for our understanding of death and judgment, even if it is buried deep in our unconscious, has a lot to do with the authenticity, courage, and fullness with which we live our lives today.

It is obvious that the apostles and the early Christian community took Jesus' promise to come again soon quite literally, and expected the Second Coming to occur in their own lifetimes. In fact, Paul had to admonish some in the Thessalonian community who had stopped all activity in expectation of Jesus' arrival to go back to work and earn their keep. (I think we will experience this again with the coming of the year 2000 when the millenarians will once again take to the mountaintops.) These early

Christians looked forward to the Final Coming with real enthusiasm. They believed God's promise to the prophet Malachi:
"But for you who fear my name, the sun of righteousness will
shine out with healing in its rays" (Ml. 3:20). They yearned with
all their heart and soul to be able to enter yet again into the
presence of Jesus, whom they loved; hence the cry from the
heart, Amen; come, Lord Jesus. Let us know the joy of your
presence!

Some biblical scholars claim that the apostles obviously misunderstood Jesus, because he did not return again in their lifetime. But there is a sense in which the apostles were right; Jesus
did return again to each of them in their own lifetime, or more
correctly, at the moment of their death. For by faith, we understand death as an entering into the presence of Jesus. And once
we pass the portals of death we are beyond time. So our own
particular judgment at the moment of death can correspond to
the general judgment at the end of time.

But if we today are perfectly honest, we will admit to ourselves that, rather than looking forward to that meeting with
Jesus with enthusiasm, many of us are filled with fear and fore-
boding and are inclined to call out, Wait, Lord Jesus! I for one
feel much more at home with the Advent collect that reads:
"Lord, remove the blindness that cannot know you. Relieve the
fear that would hide me from your sight."

My fear about meeting Jesus is based in part on the distorted
image I grew up with concerning Jesus' role as judge. I was exposed to many a Jesuit high school retreat master's traditional
talk on sin, death, judgment, and eternal hellfire (often all too
similar to the sermon on hell that James Joyce recalls in *Portrait of
the Artist as a Young Man*). Basically that talk, designed to scare
us into being good (which was the same thing as avoiding sex),
went like this: John and Mary, two good, sinless, Catholic teen-
agers, daily communicants, went to the high school prom together. Following the dance, they parked in Lovers' Lane and
"made out" in the back seat of John's father's car. Then, when
they pulled out onto the highway on their way home, crash!
They had a fatal highway accident and, since they died in mortal
sin, they went straight to hell for all eternity. There followed a
half-hour of gruesome, detailed description of what it meant to
spend eternity being burned in hellfire.

There are so many distortions and misconceptions concerning the nature of God, sin, and judgment in this kind of thinking that it is difficult to know where to begin to straighten things out. I am reminded of the story a Sicilian friend told me about the Mafia's good and bad death contracts. In a good death contract, the victim has done nothing really wrong but has just gotten in the way; therefore the hit men wait to execute him until he is leaving church on Sunday. In bad death contracts, on the other hand, the victim has done something culpable, and then the hit men wait to execute him until he is leaving his mistress's apartment on Saturday night.

In both the Jesuit retreat lecture and the Mafia contracts, it is blasphemous to think that God's judgment is mechanically tied to and determined by the exact moment in which death occurs, or that that judgment is in any way subject to human manipulation. God certainly does not condemn a victim of torture who denies his or her faith before being killed. The blasphemy is that a human could control and manipulate God's judgment.

God's judgment, if it is to be reasonable, must be a summing up of the total meaning and direction of our entire life. Maurice Blondel, the French Catholic philosopher who had a strong influence on Vatican II, put this principle very well: "I find myself condemned to life, condemned to death, condemned to eternity. If my freedom does not give final meaning to my life, I am not, as a human person I have no meaning or identity. I must be free to choose life, to choose death, to choose eternity, or I am nothing."[1] Our freedom, if it is real and not a hoax, must enter into the process of dying.

Thus for judgment to make human sense, our moment of death must, with the help of God's grace, be a moment of free choice into which the whole history of our lives and all the choices we have made enter as determining factors. We must be free to make our final choice in the presence of God.

All the good, loving, unselfish choices of our life will lead us to choose to enter into the presence of incarnate love. All our bad, unloving, selfish choices will exert pressure on us to separate ourselves from a presence that we experience as painful. And yet our final moment is one in which we freely choose and decide what meaning we will give our lives. If God truly created us free beings, then he/she must allow us this final option. This is why the moment of death has always been considered so critical: "Pray for us now and at the hour of our death."

The Jesuit retreat sermon also contains a distorted notion of what constitutes a serious offense against God. Serious sin, sin capable of separating us from Jesus for all eternity, is unlikely to be the consequence of a single act, especially an act that runs contrary to the whole direction of our lives. Rather, serious sin must be a question of our fundamental orientation within ourselves.

Finally, the Jesuit sermon places an unwarranted emphasis on the sexual nature of sin. Because of retreat talks such as this, whole generations of Christians directed their spiritual and psychic energies into a guilt-ridden effort to deny their sexual nature and needs. And since sexual needs are frequently compulsive, those who found themselves acting out their needs experienced terrible guilt and self-hatred as a result. They found themselves worshiping a God of fear who made sadistic demands.

AIDS and God's Judgment

As I stated in *The Church and the Homosexual*, we can be absolutely certain of one thing: *It is not God's will that anyone should have AIDS*. Those who interpret the AIDS epidemic as God's judgment and punishment of homosexuals reveal, first of all, their own homophobic prejudice and thinly veiled hatred of gays. Some evangelists today would have lesbians and gays revert to worship of a pagan god of fear, and they demand that we sacrifice a life of sexual intimacy in order to escape divine punishment. Those who engage in this kind of thinking reveal their ignorance of the God whom Jesus revealed. Jesus stressed that God is a loving and merciful parent who doesn't punish children, especially for something about which they have no choice.

On several occasions Jesus repudiated the notion that God inflicts physical punishment for supposed sin. When some men were killed in an accident in the temple he said, "Do you suppose these Galileans who suffered like that were greater sinners than any other Galileans? They were not, I tell you" (Lk. 13:2–3). On another occasion Jesus' disciples asked him about the fate of a man born blind: "Rabbi, who sinned, this man or his parents?" Jesus replied: "Neither he nor his parents sinned. He was born blind so that the works of God might be displayed in him" (Jn.

9:2–3). The works of God that Jesus referred to were his own mission as savior and "light of the world": he touched the blind man's eyes with spittle and his sight was restored.

In light of Jesus' teachings, the only question to be asked is, What works of God are being made manifest through the suffering and death of persons with AIDS? I certainly do not presume to have a definitive answer to this question. In fact, the answer probably varies with each individual who is affected by the AIDS crisis. However, in a spirit of good faith and trust we can believe the promise that God's love will always succeed in bringing greater good out of the evils of pain, sickness, suffering, and death. There is the "work of God" which is the personal journey that every person with AIDS makes through life and death to their own personal encounter with the God of love and their own final option.

But there is also evidence in the world and in history that God has brought good out of the evil of AIDS. An example of this, as I have mentioned, is a renewed consciousness and acceptance of our mortality and, consequently, a more intense awareness of the preciousness of life. And from a medical viewpoint we can hope for a scientific breakthrough in the treatment of viral infections. Before the AIDS crisis, I remember fearing that lesbian and gay liberation would never produce a fundamental change in social attitudes because so many exceptional gay people were so deeply closeted. AIDS has changed all this, and has caused many to come out of the closet. I think of the hundreds of gay couples whose love for each other might have remained hidden but whose selfless love and devotion unto death has now been made manifest in the AIDS wards of hospitals and hospices all over the country. I also think of Father Michael Peterson, whose open letter about his homosexuality and his fight with AIDS made a dramatic impact on all who admired his work as a psychotherapist and spiritual guide. I now have a real hope that this new public awareness of gay people and their relationships will eventually lead to full acceptance of gay couples as the full equals of their heterosexual counterparts, both in society and in the church.

The one clear and certain response that Jesus made in his day to victims of disease such as leprosy, was not one of judgment and condemnation, but rather one of compassion. When he encountered lepers he listened to them, touched them, healed them. As we read in the Gospel of Mark: "A leper came to [Jesus] and pleaded on his knees: 'If you want to . . . you can cure me.' Feeling sorry for him, Jesus stretched out his hand and touched him. 'Of course I want to!' he said, 'Be cured!' And the leprosy left him at once and he was cured" (1:40–42).

The AIDS epidemic challenges all of us to reaffirm our faith and trust in God as a loving parent in whom love and mercy, justice and peace embrace. It challenges us to do all we can to relieve both the suffering of those afflicted and the suffering of those who love them, and to hope and pray that somehow out of all this pain God will bring about greater good.

The person with AIDS needs above all else someone who is willing to touch him; someone who can listen and won't run away when he needs to vent his anger or when he needs to share his fear and despair. We should remember the question Jesus asked the disciples in the garden of Gethsemane: "Had you not the strength to keep awake one hour?" (Mk. 14:37).

The Nature of the Last Judgment

When Jesus speaks of the sins for which we will be held accountable at the Last Judgment, he does not mention impure thoughts, masturbation, or being erotically attracted to someone of the same sex, or having sexual relations with someone to whom you are not married. The sins he condemns are of quite a different nature: I was hungry and you refused to feed me; I was thirsty, naked, lonely, sick, in prison, in pain, and you refused to help me. Nowhere in his description of judgment or sin does Jesus talk about sexual acts unless those acts involved a violation of someone's person. And nowhere in the four Gospels does Jesus say a single word against homosexuality. I believe that, aside from rape, child molestation, or intentionally hurting a lover, it is very difficult for two consenting adults to commit a serious sin in a sexual gesture.

Still, every follower of Christ faces the daily challenge of choosing to exercise his or her sexuality in such a way that these energies will be used unselfishly to express love. What a better world it would be if only all the psychic energy that is now wasted in an effort to repress and deny our sexual reality could be liberated to implement the Gospel message of justice, peace, and love.

In contrast to the many distorted images of judgment that have circulated over the years, the most beautiful and accurate literary image of judgment I know occurs in C. S. Lewis's book *The Last Battle,* the seventh volume in his Chronicles of Narnia.[2] In this book, Aslan, a huge lion who is a Christ-figure and savior of his world, stands in the doorway of the stable, the same stable in which he was born. One by one the sun, moon, and stars are extinguished until there is only one source of light left: that which issues from the door of the stable. All the creatures of that world rush toward that source of light and come face to face with Aslan. Those who hated him in their lifetime and refused his rule of love are filled with loathing and dread when they see him and choose to run off into the darkness on his left. But those who loved him and kept his rule of love are filled with joy and run up to hug him and enter into the light on his right.

Notice in this scene Aslan, the God-figure, does nothing; he is what he is. It is the creatures who judge themselves according to how they chose to relate to him. Lewis's retelling of the Last Judgment makes clear the ultimate dimension of our moral freedom: whether we put God into our lives or exclude his/her loving presence depends completely on our own choice. The scene from *The Last Battle* can also help give us new insight into the meaning of our death. Death for a Christian should be understood as an entering into the presence of Jesus as the Christ. We should therefore conceive of death as a decisive and definitive act of free commitment in love, a giving of ourselves once and for all into the hands of God: "Into your hands I commit my spirit" (Lk. 23:46).

How then do we begin the process of overcoming the fears of death and judgment instilled in us as children, fears that can prevent us from living our lives fully and authentically, fears that can lead us to misunderstand an illness such as AIDS as punishment from God?

First of all, we must take a chance on God. We must believe that God is a God of love and that the god of fear is a mere idol. Then we must do everything in our power to liberate ourselves from all the pathological guilt and fear that plague us. We must see these unhealthy emotions as an insult to the true God. Finally, we must turn daily to God in prayer. I highly recommend the kind of centering prayer whereby we enter God's presence without the use of any thought or image, since for most of us all images have been contaminated with false guilt and fear. We must ask God to remove any obstacle that hides us from God's face.

In his first epistle, John tells us that perfect love casts out all fear. Listen to the fearlessness of Paul in these words from the second book of Corinthians:

> We too believe and therefore we too speak, knowing that he who raised the Lord Jesus to life will raise us with Jesus in our turn, and put us by his side and you with us. . . . That is why there is no weakening on our part. . . . For we know that when the tent that we live in on earth is folded up, there is a house built by God for us, an everlasting home not made by human hands, in the heavens. . . . Yes, we groan and find it a burden being still in this tent, not that we want to strip it off, but to put the second garment over it and to have what must die taken up into life. This is the purpose for which God made us, and he has given us the pledge of the Spirit. (4:13–5:5)

In *The Brothers Karamazov,* Father Zassima admits that no one can prove objectively that there is a life beyond the grave, and yet it is possible for us to convince ourselves of this truth. How? Through the experience of active love. Try to love your neighbor with relentless, active, effective fervor. As your love grows, you will be more and more convinced of the existence of a God of love and your own immortality. Again, as Saint Paul said: "Love does not come to an end" (1 Co. 13:8).

Listen to these words written by John, the disciple whom Jesus loved:

> Love will come to its perfection in us
> when we can face the day of Judgment without fear;
> because even in this world
> we have become as he is.
> In love there can be no fear,
> but fear is driven out by perfect love:
> because to fear is to expect punishment,
> and anyone who is afraid is still imperfect in love.
>   (1 Jn. 4:17–19)

I would like to end this chapter with a poem written by my
friend from World War II, Samuel Menashe, which I address as a
love poem to God:

> Many-named Beloved,
> listen to my praise,
> various as the seasons,
> different as the days.
> All my treasons cease
> when I see your face.[3]

19

Reflections on Mourning

Happy those who mourn: they shall be comforted.

Matthew 5:5

God is constantly calling us to new spiritual growth, but all growth involves a mourning process. In Genesis, for example, we read that Abraham, the father of all believers, must trust in God's word and let go of the old; he must leave the land of his kinfolk and his father's house and enter into a new, strange land where he will receive God's blessing. It is never too late to begin this spiritual journey; Abraham was a youthful seventy-five.

I would like to say a few words about mourning and death. We Irish are sometimes accused of having a morbid fascination with death. Every time we pick up a newspaper, we turn first to the obituaries, the "Irish scratch sheet," as we fondly call it. And yet a willingness to face death and deal with it can be a sign of spiritual health—a sign of a renewed readiness to enjoy life and to risk living fearlessly. By the same token, fear of death can also be a fear of life.

There is only one really serious question in life: Can we love on condition that the one we love must die? The unbelievers and stoics in our midst are inclined to answer no. They hold that we should never fall in love, because when the time comes the pain of loss will be too great. The person of faith, however, answers yes. For those of us who have embraced Christ's message, death has been robbed of its ultimate power. We are free to live and love in the face of death with full confidence that, through God's goodness and grace, all true love will somehow conquer the grave. It is this kind of faith that allows the Irish to turn a wake into a joyous feast.

All spiritual growth involves a mourning process, a process of grieving, a death and rebirth. Every human being is challenged to adapt to the inevitable losses that come with growth, development, aging, and death. Children must grow up and leave home. Parents grow old, become ill or infirm, and die. We ourselves, if we are lucky, grow old, and sooner or later must face final illness and death—both our own and those of the people we love.

I believe that a deep religious faith is essential to being able to grow, to accept the loss of those we love, to be able to live at peace with a human consciousness that, although it aspires to immortality, is housed in an aging body that must die. Without some sort of belief system that can give a transcendent meaning to life, no human exists without hopelessness and despair. Consequently, at every stage of life we are challenged, if we want to stay psychologically healthy, to undergo a grieving process.

Surviving the loss of love is one of the greatest and most painful challenges one can face. In this situation, as with every other kind of loss, there is both a healthy and a pathological grief process. When the grief is healthy, it brings about a gradual healing of the wound of loss and renews in us the ability to reinvest in life and love. The memory of one's love becomes peaceful, and even pleasant. Our first painful encounter with grief is often the death of a pet. We can tell that a child has successfully grieved for a lost pet when the child begins to show interest in a new puppy or kitten. If, however, the child shows no sign of ever becoming attached to another pet, we know that the grieving process has gone wrong.

It is a natural and healthy sign of grief if, a week after your loved one's funeral you find yourself setting two places for breakfast and calling to him or her to come to the table. When the reality of your loss sinks in, you will probably sit down, feel your emptiness, loneliness, and pain, and cry inconsolably. But as time goes on, these moments when the pain hits with all the freshness and intensity it had when the loss was new should begin to diminish. If, however, six months after the death of your loved one you are still setting a place for two at breakfast and holding an imaginary conversation, something has gone wrong in the grieving process and you need the professional help of a counselor or therapist. Frequently the grieving process cannot be completed because there is unconscious guilt, fear, and anger that we cannot bring into consciousness and deal with. We therefore need skilled help in order to complete the grieving process.

Because of the advances that have been made in medical knowledge, the process of dying has been considerably lengthened for many. This is often the case in AIDS-related deaths. When someone we love undergoes a drawn-out terminal illness, we may already have completed the most difficult phase of grieving before the death itself occurs. The lover, family, or friends of a person who has died from AIDS may be surprised at the peace, acceptance, and absence of great pain and sorrow they feel after their friend or relative has finally died. They should be aware that this is not a sign of a lack of feeling on their part, but rather a hard-won result of all the painful grieving they have already done.

Frequently, however, because so many of the people who die from AIDS are relatively young, the grieving process is much more difficult and protracted. It is relatively easier to grieve for the death of a loved one who has had a long and full life than for someone who dies at the age of thirty-five, the average age of the person who dies from AIDS.

The Sanskrit word for widow means "empty." The pain we feel when someone we love dies comes from this sense of emptiness. When we love someone deeply, we truly become one with that person. Our love becomes part of our core reality, our very essence. Consequently, with the death of the one we love, we experience a loss of our sense of identity, and the meaning goes out of our relationship with the world. We must redefine who we are and what the world means to us. The grieving process allows an integration of that loss into our self-consciousness.

The phases of grief differ from person to person. Frequently there is initial shock, a feeling of numbness. This is a natural protective reaction that allows us to continue functioning and gives us a breathing space to mobilize our resources in order to deal with the loss. This is usually followed by an emotional re-action and release. This is the time of pain, emptiness, tears of grief, and feelings of desperation, depression, and loneliness that sometimes seem intolerable.

It is normal during this period to feel that we don't want to live anymore. Life seems to have been robbed of all meaning and happiness, and we feel abandoned and immobilized. It is natural for thoughts of suicide to occur at this time. But religious pro-hibitions, as well as the realization that suicide would go against the wishes of our loved one, frequently prevent us from choosing this means of escape.

This stage of grief is usually accompanied by many physical symptoms. Our grief can be somatized in the form of aches, pains, fevers, and other physical symptoms. This stage can also be accompanied by psychological reactions such as intense feel-ings of panic and guilt. We may feel that we did something un-forgivable and therefore caused our loved one's death. We think, "If only I had loved better, been less selfish, had dealt with my anger, had not cheated, my loved one would still be alive." When these feelings become intense and irreconcilable, there is need again for professional bereavement counseling.

Anger is always the flip side of guilt. The bereaved will fre-quently go from feeling guilt and self-hatred to feeling over-whelming rage and anger. No one is totally free from this anger. It can be directed at one moment at oneself, then at the loved one who has died. We may feel angry with our friends, hospital per-sonnel, parents, the church, and even with God. This too is a natural, necessary, and cleansing part of the grief process.

The third phase is usually one of lassitude and exhaustion. At this point we feel the need of a protracted, healing rest. Shar-ing our joys and sorrows is the essence of a true Christian reli-gious community. The principal role of the religious community during the grieving process is to welcome the one who is griev-ing and share his or her pain.

We all have an absolute need of companionship and sharing in order to successfully complete the grieving process. We need a loving community to provide some degree of acceptance and hope and to help us maintain some contact with the living. We can still hear Jesus' plaintive call to his disciples in the garden of Gethsemane, "Had you not the strength to keep awake one hour?" (Mk. 14:37).

Gay and lesbian people frequently encounter special problems with the communal aspect of mourning. The very essence of healthy mourning lies in sharing our pain and sorrow with sympathetic friends. The framework and the rituals for doing this are built into straight society: the obituary, the wake, the funeral or church service, the family get-together, and so on. But if a gay or lesbian couple has had to keep their relationship closeted, there is no public, social outlet for their grief.

Sometimes there is even worse in store. Many newspapers do not allow the name of a gay or lesbian lover to be mentioned in an obituary. Sometimes the family of the deceased will take over the wake and funeral and not allow the lover to play the role of principal mourner or may even exclude him or her. Gays frequently find themselves exiles even at the moment of death and grieving, unable to openly share their grief, especially if the lover died of an AIDS-related illness.

One of the most painful experiences I have had as a pastor was when I was called in the early morning hours by a gay friend whose lover of twenty-five years was dying of AIDS in a Catholic hospital. His lover's family, who had come from out of town, had succeeded with the help of the hospital chaplain in having him denied all access to his lover's room. Since they had no publicly acknowledged legal relationship, he had no recourse. We walked together through the streets of downtown Manhattan crying and trying to console each other. The horror did not end there. His lover's body was shipped back to his home town for burial and, again, he was excluded. And the family took possession of all the valuable objects from the apartment they had shared for twenty-five years. Thank God, there was a gay religious community in which his grief was acknowledged and shared and his twenty-five years of love could be celebrated.

Families of those who have died from AIDS also frequently find themselves cut off from normal outlets for their grief. Returning home after their son's funeral in the big city, they find themselves isolated, with no one to share their grief.

The grieving process has a special urgency for the psychological and spiritual health of gay people and for all those who find themselves exiled from society because of their difference. I would like to recommend to all my readers that they read John Fortunato's book *Embracing the Exile: Healing Journeys of Gay Christians.*[1] Fortunato is a psychotherapist and former national president of Integrity, the national gay Episcopal organization. He stresses that grieving is something we do all the time. It always involves the five-step process that Elisabeth Kübler-Ross has described: denial, bargaining, anger, depression, and, finally, acceptance.[2] It is a process that can take place around any of life's disappointments, from not being able to turn left at a traffic light to losing someone you love. Fortunato points out that most people live according to a myth of belonging and being in control. But we lesbians and gay men, because of our difference, are outside that myth; we do not belong. How many gay people as children experience the grief of alienation from their family, when their parents are disappointed because their sons show no interest in hunting or baseball or their daughters resist being "feminine" and playing house.

From my work as a therapist, I am aware that every gay child grows up an orphan in one essential aspect. Gay adolescents are frequently rejected—and on occasion physically abused—by their peer group. Young gay men and women frequently feel isolated and try fearfully to suppress their difference in a desperate effort to belong. Because of their fear, gay adults may remain in the closet, angry at the world, involved in furtive, anonymous sex, living in constant terror that their secret will become known.

We can get stuck at any one of the stages of grieving. We can be locked into a lifelong denial of our gayness; we can get stuck at the stage of compromise, playing straight all day at work and only allowing our gayness to emerge schizophrenically on weekends; we can get stuck at the stage of anger and let cynicism and hatred, especially for our gay brothers and lesbian sisters, permeate our lives; we can get stuck at the stage of depression and never experience any joy in life.

To successfully avoid these traps, we must go through the mourning process. We must consciously deal with our feelings of denial, anger, and depression so that we may experience the joyous feelings that come when our wounds have finally healed and a peaceful acceptance replaces our pain. It is important to realize that most of us cannot accomplish this alone. We need loving friends and a loving community to help us work through this process.

Fortunato states that the psychological and spiritual growth of a gay or lesbian person depends on being able to let go of wanting to be part of the myth of belonging, of wanting to be accepted into heterosexual society, and on replacing that longing with a deepened personal process of spiritual growth:

> What gay people ultimately have to give up is attachment to rejection and the need for people (incapable or unwilling to do so) to affirm their wholeness and lovableness. It works like this: if you can't get confirmation of your wholeness and your rightful place in the universe from people and the myth, you have to look beyond them. You have no choice but to get it from someplace else, someplace deeper, someplace more cosmic.
>
> If you give up denying, fighting, and wallowing in the oppression, you stop being stuck in the mud. Off you go, down the road. You begin to see that freedom and a sense of belonging aren't to be found in the myth at all. They never were. You begin to understand what Jesus meant when he said, "Mine is not a kingdom of this world' [Jn. 18:36].[3]

To let go of the myth of belonging in this world is in some ways to have already undergone the mourning process that most people must undergo at death. The result of that process is a growing spiritual freedom to live authentically and fearlessly in this world. By deepening our spiritual life, we can turn what many see as the curse of gayness or the curse of being an exile into spiritual gold. Matthew Kelty, a Trappist monk, speaks of this aspect of gayness in his book *Flute Solo: Reflections of a Trappist Hermit:*

> Sometimes I wish I were more like others. I am aware of a difference; some insight into things, some capacity for the poetic and the spiritual which, if not exceptional—and it is not—is still strong enough to set me off from others. Nor do I hesitate to say that this has some relationship to homosexuality. For though I have never practiced it, I am well aware of an orientation that is certainly as much in that direction as the other; further, that given the knowledge, the opportunity, the circumstances, I could easily as not have gone in that direction.
>
> But people of my kind seem often so placed, the reason, as I have worked it out, that they are more closely related to the "anima" than is usual. . . . What such people yearn for is

solace in their solitude and an understanding of their fate, their destiny. . . . The man with a strong anima will always experience some inadequacy until he comes to terms with his inner spirit and establishes communion—no small achievement. Until then, he cannot act truly as a complete person, since he is not one. He will then be unable to relate in depth to others.

The unhappy experience of many is that they are unable to relate to others, not aware that their problem is a lack of communion with themselves. The blind comfort the blind, but they cannot open each other's eyes. . . .

Perhaps a healthy culture would enable those so gifted by God or nature [i.e., homosexuals] to realize their call and respond to it in fruitful ways.[4]

What must we gay people do to transform our curse into a blessing? If we find the time each day to spend in God's presence in prayer, we will develop a living, affectionate, personal relationship with God. We will then be able to recognize all the broken events of our lives—the losses, the pain, and the grief—as connected with and given meaning by the great events of God's redemptive work in Jesus. If we pray daily, we will be fully prepared for death. For if we enter freely into the presence of God, how easy it should be for those of us who have already mourned and let go of the world to enter once and for all into that presence at the moment of death. *Maranatha!* Come, Lord Jesus, come!

Almighty God, you gave your word that those who mourn will be comforted. Touch the hearts of all those who mourn because of AIDS; make them aware of your loving presence and grant them peace. Amen.

Part Seven

The Necessity of a Gay
Spiritual Community

Introduction: Lovers Gather Round

"For where two or three meet in my name, I shall be there with them" (Mt. 18:20). These astonishing words of Christ emphasize the spiritual value of community. Throughout this book we have seen the necessity of community for the spiritual liberation of gay and lesbian Christians.

Often we cling to our bad relation with the church, with God, and with each other because we are afraid that if we let go of the sick relationship, we will have no relationship at all. Better a bad parent than none; better a sadistic partner than none at all; better a homophobic church than no church at all; better a God of fear than no God at all. We are our relationships; it is the other who gives us to ourselves. Sometimes letting go of a sick relationship can feel like annihilation, so we continue to cling to it.

It is only by finding a new community, a new family, and new healthy relationships that can we find the strength to risk letting go of the old. In part 1, we saw that in order to have the strength to exorcise the god of fear and the pathology of sick religion and immature faith, we need the support of a healthy community of faith. In part 2 we saw that to let go of the demons of fear, anger, shame, guilt, and low self-esteem we need the support of a loving community. In part 5 we saw that it is only in a community of love that we are free to play and it is only in a personal relationship of love that sex can be the joyful, playful release that God intended it to be. In part 6 we saw that healthy mourning can occur only with the help of a loving community. And certainly one reason that I am able to carry on my personal ministry to gay people, and that I was able to write this book, is that I have found strength and support in the gay community, primarily in Dignity.

In this final section I would like to bear witness to what the gay religious community has meant to me personally, and to share what I see as the continuing role of that community.

20

The Role of a Gay Christian Community

My brothers [and sisters], you were called, as you know, to liberty; but be careful, or this liberty will provide an opening for self-indulgence. Serve one another, rather, in works of love, since the whole of the Law is summarized in a single commandment: Love your neighbor as yourself. *If you go snapping at each other and tearing each other to pieces, you had better watch or you will destroy the whole community.*

Galatians 5:13–15

One of the greatest blessings in my life has been the existence of Dignity, which has provided a spiritual community for many gay Catholics. Some fifteen years ago, Dignity New York held its first meeting. We were intensely aware that in all of New York, one of the gay capitals of the world, there was no ministry or organization for Catholic gays and lesbians. We decided, despite enormous anxiety, to found such a group based on the example of our Catholic gay brothers and sisters in San Diego and Los Angeles, who had formed the original Dignity chapter. And so in October 1972 we placed a small announcement in the *Village Voice* saying that an organization called Dignity, for Catholic gay men and lesbian women, would hold its first organizational meeting at Calvary Episcopal Church parish house on Gramercy Park. We had no idea what to expect, but to our astonishment over one hundred men and women showed up, and Dignity New York was off and running.

Since that first meeting we have had to change our meeting place six times. Although we have faced opposition from within and without, Dignity has survived, and whereas fifteen years ago there were only three or four chapters in the entire country, Dignity now comprises a national organization of well over a hundred chapters in the United States and Canada, and the New York chapter has helped bring into existence about ten other chapters in the metropolitan area. Organizations similar to Dignity have also sprung up in England, Australia, South America, and Spain.

What was the spirit of the founders of Dignity? We hoped against hope that somehow God would perhaps make us instruments in removing the church's blindness of sexism and heterosexism. We hoped that by working together we could find a way to integrate our religious faith and our gayness in a way acceptable to God and our church without in any way suppressing or denying our gay and lesbian reality.

We had our critics both in the gay community and the church. There were many on both sides that ridiculed us and told us we were naïve. Many in the gay community said we were foolish to hope that the church could ever be anything but homophobic and repressive for gays and lesbians. And many in the churches said that we were foolish to believe that somehow God would manifest his/her presence to us outcasts in the love that gay men and lesbian women have for each other.

And yet we trusted that Jesus would keep his word: "For where two or three meet in my name, I shall be there with them" (Mt. 18:20). We trusted that God would protect, console, and guide us, healing our blindness and relieving our fears. We understood dimly that God would manage to speak to us through our love for each other. We decided to take a chance on God.

Ultimately, our sense of dignity as lesbian women and gay men depended on a deep spiritual experience of God's love for us precisely as lesbian and gay. And we could experience that only if we could work ourselves free from self-hate and learn to love ourselves. I remember saying at the very first Dignity meeting in New York: "Dignity is not something we can give ourselves, but it *is* something we can give each other."

There is an ancient Hasidic tale that emphasizes the value of a loving community. A good rabbi asked God for a special favor: he wanted to visit both heaven and hell before he died. God granted the favor, and so he was brought to a room in the afterworld. In that room, a group of unhappy, emaciated people sat around a pot of food hanging over a fire. They were trying to feed themselves, but their efforts were in vain because their wooden spoons were too long for them to put the food in their mouths. This, he was told, was hell. Then he was taken to an identical room with a similar group of people sitting around another pot of food with the same long wooden spoons, but here there was merriment and joy. The only difference was that here they fed each other. This, he was told, was heaven. The gay Christian community must be one in which we feed ourselves by feeding each other.

The first great accomplishment of the gay Christian movement has been to bring a sense of personal dignity to thousands of gay Christians. I think most of my readers will agree that growing up Christian and gay in the United States means in most cases to grow up a profoundly wounded person. Many of us have known what it means to be an outcast from family, peers, society, church, and even God. Moreover, it was difficult for us to break out of that alienation because a conspiracy of silence left most of us believing that we were the only gay people in the world. It was through gay religious groups that many of us learned to accept ourselves. We now know from our own experience that when we meet and pray together, the Holy Spirit is in our midst with the divine gifts of healing, joy, and peace. The editor of a recent book on gay attitudes stated that if his book had come out a few years ago, it would have been a lot more self-pitying. He observes that, today, lesbians and gays seem to feel really good about themselves. Dignity, MCC, Integrity and many other gay spiritual groups have played a major role in this change in the attitude of lesbians and gays toward themselves.

As I noted in my keynote speech at the first national convention of Dignity in Hollywood, California, in 1973, this is a great time to be alive and gay and Christian. To my knowledge, this is the first time in two thousand years of Christian history that there has been a Christian gay community in which we can publicly seek each other's support in an effort to integrate our spiritual lives with our sexuality. This is a time to rejoice and be grateful, as we remember all our gay brothers and sisters, all those unmarried aunts and uncles, who lived before us and went to their graves without once being able to meet and pray with their gay brothers and sisters in Christ.

I want to bear witness to the importance that the gay spiritual community has had for me as a gay priest. At the time of my ordination some thirty years ago, my homosexual orientation was a fearful secret which I could barely acknowledge even to myself and which I had shared privately only with my spiritual director. I always feared that somehow my gayness would prevent me from being the priest I should be.

However, now that Dignity and other gay Christian groups have come into being and I have been able to celebrate the liturgy and preach and counsel my lesbian sisters and gay brothers openly, I have discovered that my gayness, rather than being a detriment, has enabled me to be of greater service. The gay Christian community has been a great blessing in my life, one for which I shall be eternally grateful to God and to my gay brothers and lesbian sisters. I pray that all gay Christians will have the chance through the ministry of gay spiritual groups to find their gayness a cause for spiritual celebration.

I think it is important at this point to renew our awareness that what we are engaged in is not a purely human task but a ministry, a work of collaboration with the spirit of God. Wherever true human liberation is taking place, whether the economic liberation of the third world, women's liberation, or gay liberation, there the spirit of God is at work. Thus we must not be surprised when serious opposition to this liberation arises, even within the church itself. All liberation entails a sharing in the cross.

The impact of the gay Christian community on the American church has been powerful. There is no question that most churchgoers are much more aware of the existence and the problems of gay Christians and take a more open, pastoral attitude toward them than was the case in the past.

Much has been accomplished and much remains to be done. In the third world the church is learning a totally new style of leadership: one that understands that power in the Christian community is in proportion to service; one that does not seek to assert hierarchical authority but rather realizes that its primary task is to listen to and be in contact with the Christian community. The various Christian gay groups represent such basic communities. These communities have offered, and should continue to offer, the opportunity for respectful dialogue with anyone in the hierarchy who is willing to listen.

The Spiritual Skill of Discernment

I would like now to address some spiritual aspects of the task that lies ahead. I see a great danger for the gay Christian community at this point in its history, a danger that can be met only by a new spiritual maturity and new spiritual depths in our ranks. I believe that anyone who wishes to be a leader in the gay Christian community must develop the spiritual skill of discernment.

Let me illustrate what I mean. A Jesuit friend of mine, who spent years in a hospital bed cut off from all possibility of ministry, finally recovered enough to be able to live in a seminary and act as spiritual father for the community. After an initial period of enthusiasm during which he did excellent work, things began to go wrong. He began to notice everything negative about the young men with whom he was working. Eventually these young men sensed his negative, critical spirit, and few continued to come to him for spiritual advice. One day, he stood at a window watching a group of young Jesuits talking with each other during the recreation period. The bell rang for the end of the period but the seminarians went right on talking. Immediately my Jesuit friend began to think: Look how disrespectful they are of the rules. They have no true religious spirit. Suddenly he had the grace to become aware that the critical, negative voice seemed to have a life of its own, a compulsive quality that was almost a form of possession. He realized that it was that voice which destroyed any positive attitude and respect he had felt toward the students and, consequently, destroyed any ability he had to be of service to them in a spirit of respect and love.

There is a basic law of the spiritual life: after an initial honeymoon period when everything seems to go well and one feels a spirit of joy and consolation, there normally follows a period of trial, a dark night of the soul. If we are doing God's work, we should expect opposition from the forces of darkness and evil. I believe every gay Christian group has experienced an initial period of joyful, hard work and enthusiastic growth followed by a period of uneasiness. The original leaders burn themselves out, objectives become hazy and confused, personalities clash, power struggles break out, there are conflicts between men and women, conflicts between those who want to appease the church and those who want to be more confrontational.

Through a communal discernment process, we must search prayerfully for the will of God. We must learn how to foster those ideas and feelings that increase our love and respect for all the members of the gay community and our love and respect for the church. We must pray and fight against being taken over by a compulsively negative, critical spirit that destroys our willingness to risk and to serve.

Discernment and Anger

As we saw in chapter 5, the most important process of communal discernment concerns how to make creative and constructive use of the anger against injustice that we legitimately feel. We gay and lesbian Christians must strive to become loving critics and critical lovers of the church. We must learn to be appropriately angry over the injustices we experience without being apologetic. We must continue to state clearly the ideals we stand for. Remember that all the great prophets, male and female, including Jesus, were angry people who channeled their anger into a fight for justice. Our anger will remain neurotic as long as we want and expect something from church authorities that they cannot or will not give us.

In order to ensure the health of the gay and lesbian community, the Christian gay community must teach us how to become self-centered in a healthy way so that we are able to take responsibility before God and our fellow humans for our choices and our lives. We must learn that we cannot live our lives to meet the expectations of others. The primary way of letting go of our anger at our parents and the church, as we have seen, is to heal the wounds they have inflicted on us. We must be a therapeutic community. If we can heal the wounds of self-hatred and self-rejection, then we can let go of the neurotic anger we feel toward those we see as having inflicted the wounds.

We must prayerfully undertake a personal reevaluation of what we have inherited, because much of what we have received from the church has been contaminated with the evil of homophobia. We must ask ourselves which of the church's values we continue to want, respect, and love; which values are compatible with who we are and arc not destructive of our dignity as persons. The basis of the communal discernment, once again, is the premise that whatever is psychologically destructive must be bad theology. Our discernment will thus perform an important service for the church, helping it to separate purely human and destructive traditions from the authentic word of God.

The primary lesson I have learned after twenty years of work with gay Christian communities all over the country is that God breaks in in the weak places. God's spirit is active in unlikely places, in the poor, broken, and humble places. The power of God is strongest in us when we admit our vulnerability, when we take risks and let go. To acknowledge that we are vulnerable is to acknowledge that we need God's help, and thus we make ourselves available to the power of God's love.

Thank you, Lord, for the gift of community! Help us to be your instrument in bringing to an end the homophobia of your church. Amen.

Conversion and the Gay Christian Community

If you are led by the Spirit, no law can touch you.

Galatians 5:18

When Jesus announced his new kingdom of God, he called for repentance and conversion.[1] To convert means literally to turn around, to stop dead in your tracks and proceed in a new direction. Jesus is telling us that humanity is somehow on the wrong path, moving away from God. What the Bible calls sin, darkness, blindness, dullness, sleep, or hardness of heart appears in our own lives as a stubborn determination to pursue our own selfish ends.

In the Bible the "from" and "to" of conversion are quite clear. Conversion is from sin to salvation, from idols to God, from slavery to freedom, from injustice to justice, from guilt to forgiveness, from a sense of being unlovable to a knowledge that we are loved, from lies to truth, from darkness to light, from self to others, from death to life. Conversion always means turning to God. We are called to respond to God from the particularities of our own personal, social, political, and sexual circumstances. The question for us as members of the Christian gay and lesbian community is: What is the turnabout in attitudes and actions to which God is calling us?

Remember the rich young man who asked Jesus what he must do to enter the kingdom of heaven? Jesus repeated the commandments: thou shalt not kill, steal, lie, commit adultery, and so on. The young man responded: "I have kept all these. What more do I need to do?" Jesus looked at him with love and said: "Go, sell what you own and give the money to the poor . . . then come, follow me" (Mt. 19:16–22). Notice that the first set of commandments Jesus mentions are all negative. They tell us what not to do, but they do not tell us what God wants of us as positive action. These commandments are based on the virtue of justice. Once our lives are just, then Jesus can turn to each of us individually and invite us into community with him, into a special form of commitment and intimacy.

Is Jesus looking at us in the Christian gay community with love and asking something more of us? I cannot answer that question for anyone but myself; each of you can find the answer in your own heart.

Conversion is always away from idolatry. Idols are those things which command an allegiance that rightly belongs to God. We resist naming our idols and cling to them. The fear that hides us from God's sight can be the fear of losing our idols. The false gods that demand our service and fidelity today are the same as those named in the Bible: wealth, power, status, pride of self, pride of nation, sexism, racism. Conversion demands that we take literally the command to love God above all else.

We must be honest with ourselves. To try to live out Christ's values would represent a radical reversal for all of us. Aggrandizement, ambition, and aggression are normal for us personally and for society. Competitiveness and jealousy enter into most of our relationships. Violence is regularly sanctioned by our culture. Selfishness mars most of our encounters. It seems to me that the gay community incarnates many of Christ's values in a striking way, especially in its gifts of empathy, compassion, and hospitality and in its renunciation of violence. Nonetheless, most of us must acknowledge honestly before God that Christ's values are not entirely ours.

On the Role of Community

The first thing Jesus did after announcing the kingdom was to gather a community. From the first calling of the disciples to the inauguration of the church at Pentecost, God's call to conversion was always simultaneously a call to community. To follow Jesus meant to share his life and to share it with others. Those who followed Jesus were given the gift of community with one another. Henceforth, they would belong to Jesus and be inextricably bound together. The Gospel was intended to create a new family in which those alienated from one another could now be made brothers and sisters in Christ. Both love and reconciliation flourished in this new community. People were no longer divided into Jew or gentile, slave or free, male or female, gay or straight. In this community the weak were protected, the stranger welcomed, those in pain were healed, the poor and the outcast were cared for and found justice. Everything was shared, joy abounded, and ordinary lives were filled with praise.

The purpose of God in Christ is to establish a new community that is a living embodiment of God's plan for the world. The witness of the Christian community is intended both to demonstrate and to anticipate the future of the world that has arrived in the person of Jesus Christ.

In our age of individualism and isolation, there is a desperate need for true community. We must not think of community as a collection of the already converted. Community is the place where we lay ourselves open to genuine conversion. In fact, it is the only environment in which the ongoing process of conversion is possible. Christian community does not exist for itself, nor is it an alternative church. Rather, it is the battleground of the movement from captivity to renewal, from conformity to transformation. As a result, a Christian community will always have to face struggle, conflict, pain, and anguish as it wages a battle with the false values around us and within us. But we also know that community can be a place of new freedom, deep healing, of great love and joy, a place to grow in truth and holiness. The community of faith enables us to resist the pressures of our culture and to genuinely proclaim something new in its midst. It is the place where the healing of our own lives as lesbian and gay Christians becomes the foundation for the healing of our gay brothers and lesbian sisters, as well as of the community at large.

We have reason to be angry at the church's failure to be a true community, especially for gay people. The more deeply we identify with the church, the deeper our anger and our feeling of betrayal. But we must never let our anger turn into bitterness and judgmental self-righteousness. I have discovered over the years that most of the problems that exist in the church exist in our own community as well. We tend to be full of the world, full of the negative aspects of our culture, and we are in a slow process of conversion.

Increasingly, we are able to identify not just with the strength of the church, but also with its many weak and broken places. The founders of the various gay Christian organizations did not set out to create a new church or denomination, since any such division would surely only reproduce the failures of the established churches. It is more important for us to speak of a new vision and a new hope for the church, a church that will have become at last a house of prayer for *all* people.

Although the biblical prophets spoke in anger to the church of their day, they spoke with broken hearts, because they knew the people who made up the church loved them and identified with them. Underlying the prophetic rebukes was a vision of a church faithful to the love of God. The prophets never spoke from arrogance, pride, bitterness, or despair. They spoke from love and hope for all the people:

Hope is rooted in love, and perfect love casts out all fear. Our love for the church should cast out all fear of the church. We lesbian women and gay men must have the same love for the church as gay children have for parents who they know love them but cannot understand or accept their gayness. This kind of love does not exclude a kind of righteous anger.

In the gay Christian community, we are still learning what it means to love. Over the past several years God has taught us much, softening our hearts, expanding our capacity to love one another and the whole of God's creation. Being human, we have not been able to avoid conflict and hurting one another. We have had to learn two essential characteristics of love: forgiveness and a humble spirit. We had to learn to forgive one another and come to know our own need for forgiveness. Without the ability to forgive, the gay and lesbian Christian community could not have survived.

In our early days we were very ambitious and thought we could take on the big issues of reforming the church and gay society. At times the big issues overwhelmed us because we forgot to attend to the simplest things, like learning to love and serving one another in our imperfections. The lesson here is a basic one. An authentic public witness requires an authentic community existence. The love, care, acceptance, justice, and peace we desire in the world must first be practiced among ourselves.

Most of us, when we first came to the gay Christian community, brought with us a spiritual emptiness. We often came with a passive and immature attitude, like children wanting to be fed. But sooner or later we had to put aside the primacy of our own needs and relinquish our narrow expectations of self-fulfillment. We had to die to the self and become part of something much larger than the self.

The most profound change that occurs in community, and the most simple, is learning the meaning of love. "I give you a new commandment; love one another; just as I have loved you" (Jn. 13:34). Love changes us. This is the central lesson of our years together. The greatest conversion within us has been the deepening of love among us, love for ourselves and for our gay brothers and lesbian sisters and for the church. People made hard and cynical by years of frustration, persecution, and discouragement are becoming gentle. Those who were tormented by paranoid fear now can reach out in trust. The strong can get in touch with their weakness and vulnerability, and the weak have found strength within themselves they didn't know they had. The freedom that comes from being loved allows us to discover many new things about God, about each other, and about ourselves.

Above all, we have learned important things about reconciliation. We all come together with different personalities, backgrounds, temperaments, spiritual and political traditions, and personal histories. The only thing many of us had in common was our desire to reconcile our gayness with our Christian faith. The only way to achieve that reconciliation was to become reconciled to one another. This must continue to be our primary commitment, for without that reconciliation there can be no real community of love. A commitment to reconciliation requires a willingness to do whatever is necessary to remain in fellowship with our gay brothers and lesbian sisters. A prime example of this has been our commitment to revise sexist language in the liturgy.

When we enter a gay Christian group, we bring with us all our faults, limits, and prejudices. When these create difficult relationships and we avoid the necessary reconciliation, we have failed. The implication is important: what we cannot reconcile in our own lives, we cannot hope to reconcile in the church or in the community at large. Over the years, we have learned much about reconciliation—how it happens, and what it demands of us in the way of caring and investment in each other.

It was in the gay and lesbian Christian community that we learned we no longer need an outside authority to affirm and authenticate us as lesbian women and as gay men. The love made available through the community provides the necessary inner authority we need to authenticate ourselves and act faithfully in the world, even while the church and society condemn us.

Finally, there is a crucial balance between vision and nurture, the prophetic and pastoral roles, in the gay Christian community. Without nurture, a community will soon exhaust itself in pursuit of its vision and lose any real quality of love. Without vision, the community forgets what love is for. Vision without nurture can be oppressive and destructive; it will place overwhelming burdens on people and result in burnout. Every gay Christian group has known such moments. Unless people are being nurtured in the vision around which their lives are called, there will be no community. Similarly, without a prophetic voice challenging us to reach out and change the world, nurture can easily degenerate into a self-serving group welfare and selfish withdrawal.

Most churches are tragically split between those who stress conversion and the inner life but have forgotten Christ's goal of transforming society, and those who emphasize Christian social action but have forgotten the necessity of conversion. Today's converts need to keep their eyes open to the social dimensions of their faith, as much as today's activists need to be spiritually open to conversion. Only then can we heal our painful divisions and witness to God's love in a true community.

The gay community stands in desperate need of the special gifts that religious gay groups can bring it. The many gay people who are still filled with self-hate and act out that hatred in self-destructive ways need a spiritual resource to which they can turn. How many gay men have bought our culture's dehumanized macho image and are engaged in self-destructive persecution of their feminine self and an active rejection of women? How many lesbian women are acting out a self-destructive anger at men? How many gay men and women are selfishly concerned with their own pleasure and profit, and do nothing to feed the hungry or clothe the naked? How many refuse to take any active role in the great issues of peace and justice in our day, even in causes that are concerned with gay rights?

God is calling us today to play a historic role in the liberation of gay people. It is a cause worthy of laying our lives on the line. And we are promised that the Holy Spirit of love will be our guide and support in this struggle.

Almighty God, send your Spirit of love into our lesbian and gay community. Help us to reconcile all differences among ourselves. Fill us with the gifts of your Spirit: love, joy, peace, patience, kindness, goodness, trust, gentleness, and self-control. We ask this through Jesus, our brother. Amen.

The Future of the Gay Christian Community

You must not accept injustice from anyone. You must be prepared to make a hidden injury visible and be prepared to die like a soldier in the process.
Mohandas K. Gandhi

After twenty years of struggling to achieve gay and lesbian liberation, where should the gay Christian groups, especially those that have tried to work within a denominational setting, go from here? Each denominational group has specific problems and opportunities, but there are general issues that confront all gay Christian groups.

The first task of every gay Christian group is to create an atmosphere in which lesbians and gays can grow psychologically and spiritually. Providing a community that is free from homophobia will continue to be necessary in most denominations for many years to come. Gay people need a loving community within which they can be out of the closet, heal their wounds, learn to accept themselves, integrate their spiritual and sexual life, nurture their spiritual development, learn to celebrate their sexuality in the presence of God, and find models for their relationships. They also need community support to find the courage to undertake the struggle for justice.

The central issue for many groups is the extent to which one should continue to work primarily within one's denomination. Lutherans Concerned, for example, issued a document entitled *A Call for Dialogue: Gay and Lesbian Christians and the Ministry of the Church*. The gay and lesbian Lutherans who wrote this document offer it

> in commitment to a church we will not abandon, as it labors to perfect its understanding of and ministry with lesbians and gay people. We call the church to dialogue. Lutherans Concerned, in its ministry to individuals, pastors and congregations, offers its fullest resources for pastoral care and counsel, study and theological discussion.[1]

It is encouraging that these gay Lutherans feel there is still hope for fruitful dialogue within their denomination.

A different problem faces Dignity and the Roman Catholic church. In its recent pronouncements the Vatican has made it clear that it sees no possibility of dialogue on the issue of homosexuality. By refusing to engage in official dialogue and by denying Dignity the basic right to meet as a group on church property, the Vatican has demonstrated that the church will deal with lesbian and gay members only as isolated individuals who will consent to attend heterosexist services and who are willing to admit that their sexual feelings and interpersonal love constitute "an objective disorder tending to evil."

At its 1987 national convention in Miami, Dignity refused to back down in the face of the Vatican's opposition. It reaffirmed its position that there are morally good gay and lesbian sexual relationships. In *A Pastoral Letter on Sexual Ethics: A Preliminary Study Document*, published in 1987, Dignity concludes with these words:

> We are His disciples, the gay and lesbian People of God in the Body of Christ, part of the Catholic tradition. While we continue to identify ourselves as Catholic, we emphatically, though respectfully, dissent from the teachings of Church officials regarding homosexuality. We do so, not out of a spirit of defiance but because of what we have seen and heard. We continue to explore how to express our sexuality in an ethically responsible manner consonant with the teachings of Christ. We do so by reflecting on our personal expe-

rience and learning from those who are engaged in similar reflection. We do so by praying together and celebrating Christ's presence in our midst in Word and Sacrament. We do so under the guidance of Christ's spirit, who will lead us ultimately into the fullness of truth.

Fortunately, not all dioceses have carried out the Vatican order to evict Dignity. Yet even in those dioceses where Dignity has been expelled from church-owned property, the chapter continues to meet, usually in an Episcopal or Unitarian church that has made them welcome or in the local lesbian and gay community center. These chapters plan to continue as a community of worship in exile, meeting the needs of their members and discerning how they can best engage their church in dialogue. They await the moment, or *kairos*, when the Holy Spirit will once again penetrate the closed hearts of authority.

The most astute assessment of the role of the gay Christian community in a denominational setting that I am aware of, is Gary Comstock's keynote address, *Aliens in the Promised Land?*, given before the national meeting of the United Church of Christ Lesbian/Gay Coalition on July 5, 1986. Comstock began his address by stating that he felt he was nearing the end of a long process of trying to find a place for himself and other gay men and lesbians in the United Church of Christ. He pointed out that, despite years of effort at dialogue, the church remained a place "where I feel defensive and least encouraged to share the meaningful and intimate parts of my life. The Church remains for me the place where the lump still tightens in my throat, where my stomach still knots in anticipation of rejection and difficulty, where I find myself ill at ease." This was still the case, Comstock asserted, in a church that supposedly had one of the most liberal policies concerning lesbians and gays.

Comstock was also troubled about his church's lack of action on issues of social justice: "While the church should be the place in which and from which people join together to make justice, as a gay man I find that most of my struggles against oppression of lesbians and gay men have had to be waged *against* my denomination, instead of in concert with it". Comstock pointed out that on the issues of AIDS, homophobic violence, civil rights, and the Supreme Court decision on sodomy, his church had remained silent, and stated that much of the energy for justice among gay church people had been drained off in fights within the denomination. He pointed out that, although he had all the appropriate credentials, degrees, experience, and references, his denomination would not ordain him. He even met with search committees that accepted him with enthusiasm, only to reverse their decision when he told them that he was gay.

The church, Comstock believes, has no trouble in seeing gay people as victims in need of help. However, it has great difficulty in accepting gays and lesbians as fully competent people who can respond to the needs of others. For heterosexuals to accept gay people as capable of aiding the growth and happiness of the community at large, requires a major change in the general perception of gay people's position, power, and influence. They must accept us as people of equal worth within the religious community. So far, most congregations have refused to take that step.

Many fully qualified gay and lesbian priests, ministers, and religious have given up struggling with their church and have chosen instead to engage in serious pastoral work in nontraditional settings. Programs for both young and old gay people, anti-violence projects, AIDS projects, gay and lesbian rights organizations, counseling services, and so on are frequently staffed by people who were trained for the ministry but were rejected by their seminary, church, or religious order, or who chose to leave in order to provide direct service to gay people. I am personally aware of many gay ministers, priests, and religious who had no trouble leading celibate lives and yet who have left their denomination because they could no longer in good conscience be identified with the unjust homophobia of their church. Comstock states:

> It is as if we have developed a ministry (without our denominations' approval) that is actually more in line with the ministry Jesus spoke of in chapter 25 of the Gospel of Matthew. What has been a priority for us has been to respond to the needs of the needy, to liberate the oppressed. I would suggest that many of us have already chosen to locate our ministries where a church is alive, caring, ministering, open and thriving.

In many denominations, significant progress has been made in welcoming and integrating lesbians and gays into the community. For example, the Methodists have "reconciling congregations" whose purpose is to affirm the participation of lesbians and gay men and "heal the gulf between the United Methodist Church and its gay and lesbian members." Presbyterians have "More Light" communities, which have a similar goal. Riverside Church in New York has issued a statement affirming lesbians and gay men as full members of the congregation.

Many churches will now accept openly lesbian and gay candidates for ordination into the ministry. Most recently, the presiding bishop of the Lutheran church accepted three gay candidates. However, the mistaken notion that Scripture condemns loving sexual activity between two persons of the same sex has led almost all the churches, even those that accept married clergy, to officially demand a commitment to celibacy from lesbian and gay candidates. (There are, however, a few dioceses where clergy involved in open lesbian and gay relationships are tolerated.) For the most part this position forces lesbian and gay clergy to keep their relationships hidden and to live in constant fear of discovery and rejection.

Gary Comstock concluded his United Church of Christ address by stating that it is time for the gay and lesbian spiritual community to define itself independently and abandon the need to be approved by a particular denomination.

> If the UCC cannot find a way to ordain us, to take our struggle as seriously as it does its concerns for nuclear disarmament, apartheid, the family, the aged, racism, sexism and Central America, then we shall have to ordain ourselves, form our own churches, recognize ourselves, and interact with the world with a new independence.

Comstock feels that the gay and lesbian community has developed the strengths it needs to live, learn, and love freely, without the permission or approval of a denomination.

> While an active, on-going critique of its practices is necessary, investing ourselves totally or primarily in its response to us is not. If our denomination is not ready to join us in the task of freeing the captives from heterosexism and homophobia, perhaps it is time to bring closure to a relationship that is not mutual and reciprocal. Perhaps in time they will join us.

I do *not* agree with Comstock that gay Christian groups should form their own church. On the contrary, I believe that gay Christian communities should refuse to allow themselves to be separated from their parent church, and should instead remain within it as loyal opposition. What I do agree with, however, is the assertion that the only reasonable way to stay in a denomination is as healthy, independent adults ready to deal with our church from a position of strength, courage, and autonomy, and not from a position of infantile weakness, fear, and dependence.

One notable model for gay spiritual community is the Metropolitan Community Church. Brought into existence by the Reverend Troy Perry to meet the spiritual needs of the gay and lesbian community, the MCC is one of the fastest-growing denominations in the country. The MCC has a congregation in every major American city and provides a warm, loving, and healing community that reaches out to all lesbians and gay men, and especially to those who cannot tolerate the homophobia of most traditional churches.

It is evident from the examples cited in this chapter that gay and lesbian Christian groups face two major challenges. The first is to continue the struggle to confront and change the homophobia of the various denominations and to win the right to complete participation and acceptance as gay people living in gay relationships. As Rosemary Reuther observed, our living room liturgies will disappear with the death of their participants, but any change in the church's teachings, practice, and structures will last for all future generations.

The second challenge is to provide a spiritual community that can provide for all the needs of lesbians and gays that the churches, because of their homophobia, have failed to meet. The gay and lesbian spiritual community needs to provide the human and spiritual setting where the coming-out process outlined in chapter 7 can be accomplished. The gay Christian community should also recognize, ordain, and mission gays and lesbians to their specific ministry within the gay and lesbian community. This missioning could take the form of a new understanding of confirmation as it applies to the gay community. Confirmation has always been understood as the sacrament of adulthood and maturity: one receives from God and the community the gifts of the Holy Spirit—gifts of patience, courage, and fortitude—in order to take one's place in the world as an adult.

The first confirmation took place while the apostles were still in hiding. The immediate effect of their experience was to enable them to face their fears and act courageously in the world.

We must find the strength and grace to fight the injustice of homophobia and to make manifest all the invisible injustices visited daily on gay people. Gay people have a special need for a pentecostal outpouring of the gifts of the Holy Spirit so that, our wounds having been healed, we can go forth with courage and maturity to serve God by serving each other.

Almighty God, our Father and Mother, pour out your spirit on the gay Christian community! Fill us with the special gifts of the Holy Spirit, gifts of discernment, courage, and maturity, so that, knowing your will, we may have the strength to seek justice fearlessly for our lesbian sisters and gay brothers. Help us to confront our churches as loving critics and critical lovers. Above all, fill us with the spirit of love, so that we may love each other and continue to love those who are our enemies. We ask this grace through Jesus Christ. Amen.

Epilogue:
A Liberation Spirituality Based on Gay and Lesbian Experience

My central purpose has been to explore the spiritual and theological dimensions of gay and lesbian liberation. For his book on the spiritual journey of the poor of South America, Gustavo Gutierrez took as a title a famous statement by Saint Bernard of Clairvaux about the spiritual life: "We drink from our own wells." Spirituality, Gutierrez writes, is like living water that springs up from the very depths of the experience of faith. To drink from your own well means to reflect on your own unique encounter with God. This has nothing to do with abstract opinions, convictions, ideas, dogmas, and so on. What I am talking about is the person of faith's real first-hand experience of the presence of God in her or his life, not an experience mediated through family or church. I believe in a God who actively communicates with us corporately and as individuals. I believe that God can be met personally, and that our adult faith must be based ultimately on that personal encounter.

In the "Rules for the Discernment of Spirits" of his *Spiritual Exercises,* Ignatius Loyala claimed that God is in continuous personal dialogue with those who are seeking the divine presence and that God speaks to us principally not through our minds, but through our feelings. If we have made a fundamental commitment to God and if what we are choosing and doing is in accord with God's will, we will experience consolation, that is, a deep feeling of peace and joy and a strengthening of trust, faith, and hope. By the same token, if we are experiencing feelings of desolation and turmoil, this is a sign from God that something is amiss. Our spiritual life and its development depend on our learning to be keenly aware of these feelings, to trust them, and let them guide us through life. We should engage in both an individual and a communal process of discernment.

One of the basic premises of this book is that there is a unique gay and lesbian experience of God. This special experience was given expression in a recent theological statement issued by Lutherans Concerned:

> Indeed, gay and lesbian Christians, like any other Christians who have had deep encounters with the word of the Gospel, are able to see the word speaking directly and profoundly to their own experience. Lesbians and gay men will be bold enough to offer new insight into the Gospel to the whole community of Christ. . . . Ultimately, lesbian and gay people within the church will make a great contribution to the construction of relational ethics and to evangelical outreach, which we pray will draw many others who are estranged, alienated or unloved, to Jesus Christ, to the household of faith, and into the reconciliation which has begun.

This statement mentions two of the many special gifts that the gay community can offer the human community at large. The first is the "development of relational ethics." The procreative ethic of the past has now become positively harmful. We have need instead of a new understanding of sexual relations based on an interpersonal ethics of love based on the equality of the partners. Since gay couples have been obliged to form such an ethic, there is a providential aspect to the emergence of a Christian gay community at this point in history. The second gift that gay people are making to the churches is to challenge them to open up to all members of the human family, especially those who are sexually different.

After over twenty years of ministry with thousands of gay people as priest and psychotherapist, I am convinced that a unique and vibrant spirituality is springing up among gay Christians. I also believe that this spirituality has been given a special quality by the experience of suffering that has resulted from their alienation from and persecution by the church.

But as John Fortunato has observed, almost nothing has been written about the journey of spiritual awakening for people who are gay. Gay people have a desperate need to understand their lives and experiences in light of Scripture. We have a need to hear the story of others who have undertaken the gay spiritual journey with its unique perils and opportunities. One of the tragedies of gay people in the past has been their enforced isolation from one another and their inability to pass on a history and legacy to younger generations. As Father Tom Clarke observes in his article in the book *Tracing the Spirit:* "To be deprived of one's story is the most ruthless form of oppression. Individuals, groups, peoples who society through racism, sexism, classism has denied ownership of a distinctive story will inevitably be tempted to despair of themselves." [1] A central task in our journey of spiritual liberation must be to break through our imposed isolation and to share our experience with other gay and lesbian people.

One of the most serious obstacles to spiritual liberation and healthy spirituality for gay people has been the church itself. The most recent example of this has been the efforts of the Roman Catholic hierarchy to drive Dignity out of the church and keep its gay members isolated or bound together in self-hatred in organizations such as Courage.

Many aspects of the spirituality of liberation that Gutierrez deals with in *We Drink from Our Own Wells* are also present in lesbian and gay spirituality. In his foreword to Gutierrez's book, Henri Nouwen points out how the poor and marginalized in Latin America have realized that the forces of death and oppression have made them strangers in their own land: "They recognize more clearly the ways in which they are bound by hostility, fear and manipulation and they have gradually come to understand the evil structure that victimizes them." [2] Similarly, gay and lesbian Christians are gradually becoming aware of the paranoid manipulations, fear, and hostility that surround them; they have begun to confront the evil structures that victimize them disguised as morality and the will of God. They have come to recognize the messages they receive from society and the church as polluted waters. "With the new self-consciousness," Nouwen continues, "the poor have broken into history and have rediscovered that the God whom they have worshiped for centuries is not a God who wants their poverty but a God who wants to liberate them from the forces of death and offer them life in all its dimensions."[3] Gays and lesbians have also begun the process of breaking into history with a new positive self-consciousness that has dispelled the shadow of guilt and self-hatred.

A unique obstacle to gay liberation is internalized homophobia. The attitudes that victimize gays are frequently taken in from the family and the church in earliest childhood. These evils are built into the very structure of heterosexual society and thus can easily become part of the gay person's identity. As a result the gay or lesbian adult may be plagued by shame and self-hatred.

Even the words of Scripture have become contaminated by homophobia. This was illustrated in a striking way when the Catholic Church released a new translation of the Bible in which a very obscure word in Paul's Epistle to the Colossians (*arsenokoitai*) was retranslated as "practicing homosexuals" (this group is listed among those excluded from the kingdom of heaven). Two thousand years later, a word that Paul probably used to designate some form of dehumanized, self-destructive, and lustful same-sex male behavior has been translated as though it were consciously intended to condemn a loving sexual relationship between two persons of the same sex, a situation which Paul, with his strict Jewish background, probably never imagined could exist.

The result, as we have seen, is that the process of self-liberation for gay people simultaneously becomes a process of alienation from one's family and from the human church. As a psychotherapist, I am keenly aware that as my lesbian and gay clients grow in psychic health, as they free themselves from self-hate and become more accepting and affirming of their sexual nature, they frequently come into greater conflict with both society and the church.

An example of this can be found in a communication from the Congregation for Seminaries in which Cardinal William Baum advises seminary heads to accept as candidates for ordination only those gay men whose homosexuality is "egodystonic." This word is taken from the official classification of mental disorders of the American Psychological Society, and implies that such individuals are so in conflict with their sexual orientation that they can be classified as mentally ill. Cardinal Baum advises that any candidate whose homosexuality is "egosyntonic"—in other words, any candidate who accepts his gayness—be rejected. The cardinal is essentially suggesting that there is no place in the church for healthy, self-accepting gays.

As gay people achieve greater self-consciousness and health, they will face increasing opposition. Thus they have a special need for a personal spirituality based on their direct experience of God. The self-hating gay or lesbian fits into society and the church. The self-loving gay or lesbian becomes the "real enemy" who must be destroyed.

Because of all the injustice with which we still have to contend, our efforts to achieve gay liberation must include a struggle against oppressive authority. As one liberation theologian has pointed out, liberation from oppression is a true value of the Gospel. We must become aware that Christian freedom comes from within through the spirit of Christ, and we must realize that that freedom is something to be claimed, not something that is granted by external authority. We must listen to the spirit within us, listen to the voice of the oppressed around us, and then act for human rights and equality.

We must remember, too, that we cannot merely accept the alienation that has been forced upon us. The spirit of God is moving powerfully within our gay Christian communities, and we are discovering that the God we worship is not a God who wants us to hate ourselves but a God who wants to liberate us from the forces of fear and death and offer us life in all its dimensions, including genuine personal relations of love that find expression in positive sexual communion. This healing spiritual journey can take place only in a sharing community. The church has always striven to isolate gay people and continues to do so. All those engaged in the gay struggle for liberation are aware of the importance of warm, affectionate, caring relationships. Gay spiritual community is based not on a political struggle against a common enemy or a drive for power but rather on a special personal encounter with God's love. It is the abundance of God's love, poured out in a special way to gay people, that sets them free to work to create a human community of joy, peace, and true love for everyone.

One of the special insights into the Gospels that that gay and lesbian experience has given us is an extraordinary sense of the mature fullness of the person of Christ. Christ transcended all the heterosexist role models of his day. Lesbians and gays can be particularly sensitive to this androgynous fullness, and thus can be extraordinarily free to realize that fullness in their lives. Gay spirituality is truly based in the spirituality of Jesus, which is a spirituality of universal love: "my house will be called a house of prayer for all the peoples" (Is. 56:7). Gays have an extraordinary freedom to love and give, even within a society and a church that misunderstands, distrusts, hates, and persecutes them. Gay spirituality calls for an extraordinary ability to live out what many see as the most difficult commandment of all: Love your enemy; do good to those who hate you.

Gay spirituality is of its nature very dynamic; it is one of the new movements of the Holy Spirit in the human family. To be able to be attentive to this movement requires an ear that has been well trained by Scripture. A constant dialogue is necessary between the "old knowing" of Scripture and tradition and the "new knowing" that comes from the concrete daily experience of the gay people of God. Since the gay experience has been one of flagrant injustice and moralistic condemnation, the discussion will frequently take the form of confrontation. This dialogue will demand that both church and society have the humility to recognize that structural evils have been a part of religious tradition for the past two thousand years.

There is a depth to our struggle that is hard to grasp. It is above all else a struggle for the freedom to love; it is a struggle to break free from all the obstacles to love and intimacy. This victory will be not just for gay people, but for the entire human community. Every person will be free to grow up with less anxiety concerning their sexual feelings and less need to repress or deny them.

Gay spirituality is centrally involved with the virtue of trust. As we have seen, this struggle is first of all a struggle to achieve self-trust, a struggle to believe what God is saying to us directly through our experiences, a struggle to see ourselves as persons with divine dignity and responsibility, to see our gayness as a blessing rather than a curse. We must learn to celebrate our gay existence.

Finally, I would like to say a few words about what the past twenty years of working with the gay community has meant to me. The chapters of this book were forged out of my own personal journey of liberation as a wounded healer. Originally, all I had to bring to my gay sisters and brothers were my own wounds: my self-hate, guilt, anger, and fear. It was in the profound sharing of my pain that I began to experience liberation. Out of that process came a renewed power to love, to throw off self-pity, cynicism, and despair, to give myself joyously to the work of God's kingdom and above all else to experience my gayness as a blessing. Deo gratias: thanks be to God. And a profound thank-you to all the lesbians and gay men who honored me by sharing deeply their life's journey with all its pain and sorrow and all its joy and hope.

Notes

Preface

1. James B. Nelson, *Between Two Gardens: Reflections on Sexuality and Religious Experience* (New York: Pilgrim Press, 1983).

2. In *Tracing the Spirit: Communities, Social Action, and Theological Reflection,* ed. James E. Hug, S.J. (Mahwah, N.J.: Paulist Press, 1983), 18–50.

3. Ibid., 22.

4. Gustavo Gutierrez, *A Theology of Liberation,* trans. Sr. Caridad Inda and John Eagleson (New York: Orbis Books, 1973), 208.

5. The material in this section was originally published in my article "Homosexuality: Challenging the Church to Grow," in the series "After the Revolution: The Church and Sexual Ethics," *The Christian Century,* 11 March 1987.

6. John J. McNeill, *The Church and the Homosexual,* revised and expanded edition (Boston: Beacon Press, 1988).

7. These thoughts are discussed at length in my article "Homosexuality, Lesbianism and the Future: The Creative Role of the Gay Community in Building a More Humane Society," in *A Challenge to Love: Gay and Lesbian Catholics in the Church,* ed. Robert Nugent (New York: Crossroad, 1984).

8. "Taking a Chance on Love," by J. LaTouche, Ted Fetter, and Vernon Duke, © 1940 (renewed 1968) by Miller Music Corp.; rights assigned to SBK Catalog Partnership. All rights controlled and administered by SBK Miller Catalog, Inc. International copyright secured. All rights reserved. Used by permission.

Introduction to Part 1

1. C. G. Jung, *The Collected Works,* trans. R. F. C. Hull (New York: Pantheon, 1959), vol. 9, part 1, pp. 86–87.

2. Mark Thompson, *Gay Spirit: Myth and Meaning* (New York: St. Martin's Press, 1987).

Chapter 1: Developing a Mature Faith Life

1. Heinz Heger, *The Men with the Pink Triangle,* trans. David Fernbach (Boston: Alyson Publications, 1980), 41–43.

Chapter 3: Pathological Religion and Healthy Religion

1. These reflections were originally presented at the Second Annual Conference on Culture, Race, and Ethnicity in Group and Family Therapy held at New York University, March 1987.

2. W. Robert Beavers, *Psychotherapy and Growth: A Family Systems Perspective* (New York: Brunner/Mazel, 1977).

Introduction to Part 2

1. William A. Berry and William J. Connolly, *The Practice of Spiritual Direction* (Minneapolis: Seabury Press, 1982), 8.

Chapter 5: Dealing with Anger

1. *New York Times,* 18 June 1984.

2. Ibid.

3. John E. Boswell, *Christianity, Social Tolerance, and Homosexuality: Gay People in Western Europe from the Beginning of the Christian Era to the Fourteenth Century* (Chicago: University of Chicago Press, 1980).

Chapter 6: Liberation from Fear

1. Henri J. Nouwen, *Lifesigns: Intimacy, Fecundity, Ecstasy in Christian Perspective* (New York: Doubleday, 1986).

2. Ibid., 15.

3. Jim Forrest, "Be Not Afraid," *Sojourners,* December 1983, 14–15.

4. Nouwen, *Lifesigns,* 16.

5. Alice Miller, *For Your Own Good: Hidden Cruelty in Child-Rearing and the Roots of Violence* (New York: Farrar, Straus and Giroux, 1983).

6. Chris Glaser, "AIDS and the A-Bomb Disease: Facing a Special Death," *Christianity and Crisis* 47, no. 13 (September 1987): 311–14.

7. Robert Jay Lifton, *Death in Life: Survivors of Hiroshima* (New York: Basic Books, 1982).

8. Nouwen, 108.

9. Ibid., 38–40.

Chapter 7: Lifting the Burden
of Guilt, Shame, and Self-Hate

1. W. Ronald Fairbairn, *Psychoanalytic Studies of the Personality* (New York: Methuen, 1966).

2. In D. W. Winnicott, *The Maturational Process and the Facilitating Environment: Studies in the Theory of Emotional Development* (New York: International Universities Press, 1965).

3. Ibid., 104.

4. W. Robert Beavers, *Psychotherapy and Growth: A Family Systems Perspective* (New York: Brunner/Mazel, 1977).

5. Jean-Paul Sartre, *Being and Nothingness: An Essay on Phenomenological Ontology,* trans. Hazel E. Barnes (New York: Washington Square Press, 1956).

6. Edmund Bergler, *Homosexuality: Disease or Way of Life?* (New York: Macmillan, 1962).

7. Eli Coleman, "Developmental Stages of the Coming Out Process," in *Homosexuality and Psychotherapy: A Practitioner's Handbook of Affirmative Models,* no. 4 in the series Research on Homosexuality, ed. John C. Gonsiorek (Falls Church, Va.: Howarth Press, 1982), 31–44.

8. See P. Fischer, *The Gay Mystique: The Myth and Reality of Male Homosexuality* (New York: Stein and Day, 1972), 249.

9. Coleman, "Developmental Stages," 34.

10. If one does choose to engage in sexual activity during this period, one must be intensely aware of the dangers of unsafe sex and know how to practice safer sex. One must also make a prudent judgment as to whether the possibility of developing an intimate relationship justifies the health risks involved.

11. Paul Tournier, *Guilt and Grace: A Psychological Study* (San Francisco: Harper and Row, 1962).

12. Ibid., 171.

Introduction to Part 3

1. In this introduction I wish to acknowledge my indebtedness to Matthew Fox's chapter "The Spiritual Journey of the Homosexual . . . and Just About Everybody Else," in *A Challenge to Love: Gay and Lesbian Catholics in the Church,* ed. Robert Nugent (New York: Crossroad, 1983).

Chapter 8: Trusting in God

1. Matthew Fox, "The Spiritual Journey of the Homosexual . . . and Just About Everybody Else," in *A Challenge to Love: Gay and Lesbian Catholics in the Church,* ed. Robert Nugent (New York: Crossroad, 1983), 197.

Chapter 10: Reconciliation and God's Presence

1. Edward Schillebeeckx, *Christ: The Experience of Jesus as Lord* (New York: Crossroad, 1983).
2. Ibid., 785.

Introduction to Part 4

1. John J. McNeill, *The Church and the Homosexual,* revised and expanded edition (Boston: Beacon Press, 1988).
2. *New York Times,* 1 July 1986, A18.
3. Gustavo Gutierrez, *We Drink from Our Own Wells: The Spiritual Journey of a People,* trans. Matthew J. O'Connell (New York: Orbis Books, 1984).

Chapter 11: The Spirit of Hospitality

1. Henri Nouwen, *The Wounded Healer: Ministry in Contemporary Society* (Garden City, N.Y.: Image Books, 1979), 89.

Chapter 12: The Virtue of Compassion

1. Harold Searles, "The Patient as Therapist to His Analyst," in *Tactics and Techniques in Psychoanalytic Therapy,* vol. 2, *Countertransference* (Northvale, N.J.: Jason Aronson, 1975), 95–149.
2. Ibid.
3. Alice Miller, *Prisoners of Childhood: How Narcissistic Parents Form and Deform the Emotional Lives of Their Gifted Children* (New York: Basic Books, 1981), 22–27.

Chapter 13: The Freedom to Play

1. Johan Huizinga, *Homo Ludens: A Study of the Play Element in Culture* (Boston: Beacon Press, 1955).
2. J. D. Salinger, *Raise High the Roof Beam, Carpenters, and Seymour: An Introduction* (New York: Bantam Books, 1971), 202.

Chapter 14: This Is My Body

1. Human Rights Campaign Fund Dinner, Waldorf-Astoria Hotel, New York City, 10 October 1984.

2. I highly recommend Theodore Isaac Rubin's *Compassion and Self-Hate: An Alternative to Despair* (New York: Ballantine, 1975).

3. Sebastian Moore, review of *The Feast of Love: Pope John Paul II on Human Intimacy* by Mary G. Dworkin (Chicago: Loyola University Press, 1986), published in *Commonweal,* 7 November 1986, 600–601.

4. James Nelson, *Embodiment: An Approach to Sexuality and Christian Theology* (Minneapolis: Augsburg Press, 1978).

Chapter 15: Sex as Play

1. James Nelson, *Between Two Gardens: Reflections on Sexuality and Religious Experience* (New York: Pilgrim Press, 1983).

2. Helmut Gollwitzer, *Song of Love: A Biblical Understanding of Sex* (Philadelphia: Fortress Press, 1978).

3. Ibid., 25–26.

4. Ibid., 40.

5. Ibid., 38.

6. John J. McNeill, *The Church and the Homosexual,* revised and expanded edition (Boston: Beacon Press, 1988), 205.

7. Ibid., 212.

Chapter 16: The Relationship between Mary, the Mother of God, and the Gay and Lesbian Community

1. W. Robert Beavers, *Psychotherapy and Growth: A Family Systems Perspective* (New York: Brunner/Mazel, 1977).

Introduction to Part 6

1. John Snow, *Mortal Fear: Meditations on Death and AIDS* (Cambridge, Mass.: Cowley Publications, 1987), 36–37.

2. Ibid., 35.

Chapter 17: The Christian Understanding of Death, Resurrection, and Time

1. Ernest Becker, *The Denial of Death* (New York: Free Press, 1973), 262.

2. Edward Schillebeeckx, *Christ: The Experience of Jesus as Lord* (New York: Crossroad, 1983), 793.

3. John E. Fortunato, *AIDS: The Spiritual Dilemma* (San Francisco: Harper and Row, 1987), 85–86.

4. Pierre Teilhard de Chardin, *Hymn of the Universe* (New York: Harper and Row, 1969), 150.

Chapter 18: Reflections on Judgment

1. Maurice Blondel, *L'Action: Essai d'une critique de la vie et d'une science de la pratique* (Paris: Félix Alain, 1893), vii. See also John J. McNeill, *The Blondelian Synthesis: A Study of the Influence of German Philosophical Sources on the Formation of Blondel's Method and Thought* (Leiden: E. J. Brill, 1966), 121.

2. C. S. Lewis, *The Last Battle* (New York: Macmillan, 1986).

3. Samuel Menashe, *Collected Poems* (Orono, Me.: National Poetry Foundation, University of Maine, 1986).

Chapter 19: Reflections on Mourning

1. John Fortunato, *Embracing the Exile: Healing Journeys of Gay Christians* (San Francisco: Harper and Row, 1984).

2. Elisabeth Kübler-Ross, *On Death and Dying* (New York: Macmillan, 1969).

3. Fortunato, *Embracing the Exile,* p. x.

4. Matthew Kelty, *Flute Solo: Reflections of a Trappist Hermit* (Garden City, N.Y.: Doubleday, 1980).

Chapter 21: Conversion and the Gay Christian Community

1. In this chapter I wish to acknowledge my indebtedness to Jim Wallis's book *Call to Conversion: Recovering the Gospel for These Times* (San Francisco: Harper and Row, 1983). Jim is the founder of an ecumenical community in Washington, D.C., called Sojourners, a community committed to living out Gospel values in a radical way. I now realize that many of the spiritual insights into conversion and community that Jim derived from his years of experience with Sojourners are applicable to our experience in the Christian gay and lesbian community.

Chapter 22: The Future of the Gay Christian Community

1. *A Call for Dialogue: Gay and Lesbian Christians and the Ministry of the Church.* Statement issued by Lutherans Concerned/North American Task Force on Theology, October 1985 (P.O. Box 10461, Fort Dearborn Station, Chicago, Ill., 60610-0461).

Epilogue: A Liberation Spirituality
Based on Gay and Lesbian Experience

1. Thomas E. Clarke, S.J., in *Tracing the Spirit: Communities, Social Action, and Theological Reflection,* ed. James E. Hug (Mahwah, N.J.: Paulist Press, 1983), 18–50.

2. Henri Nouwen, in Gustavo Gutierrez, *We Drink from Our Own Wells: The Spiritual Journey of a People,* trans. Matthew J. O'Connell (New York: Orbis Press, 1984), xvi.

3. Ibid.